WILL MARRY
FOR FOOD, SEX, AND LAUNDRY

adamsmedia

avon, massachusetts

how to get him—and how to keep him

BY SIMON OAKS

WILL MARRY
FOR
FOOD, SEX, AND
LAUNDRY

Published by
Adams Media, a division of F+W Media, Inc.
57 Littlefield Street, Avon, MA 02322. U.S.A.
www.adamsmedia.com

ISBN 10: 1-59869-790-0
ISBN 13: 978-1-59869-790-2

Printed in the United States of America.

J I H G F E D C B A

Library of Congress Cataloging-in-Publication Data
is available from the publisher.

This publication is designed to provide accurate and authoritative information with regard to the subject matter covered. It is sold with the understanding that the publisher is not engaged in rendering legal, accounting, or other
professional advice. If legal advice or other expert assistance is required, the
services of a competent professional person should be sought.
——From a *Declaration of Principles* jointly adopted by a Committee of the
American Bar Association and a Committee of Publishers and Associations

Many of the designations used by manufacturers and sellers to distinguish
their product are claimed as trademarks. Where those designations appear in
this book and Adams Media was aware of a trademark claim, the designations
have been printed with initial capital letters.

This book is available at quantity discounts for bulk purchases.
For information, please call 1-800-289-0963.

For all the ladies in my life.

May you never all gang up on me at once.

contents

acknowledgments

My thanks go to Brian Thornton. This book wouldn't exist without you. I'll be forever in your debt—but don't think you're getting any royalties, Brian.

Thanks also go to Paula Munier for thinking I was the man for the job. I hope this book does your faith justice.

Thanks to Brendan O'Neill for keeping me in touch with my feminine side.

Finally, thanks to all my lady friends who were only too willing to tell me what was wrong with my half of the species. I've withheld your names out of respect, and fear of reprisals.

boys will be boys

As we've been told over and over, men and women really do seem to be from different planets. That's a fair statement—and pretty obvious. Men *are* different from women and women *are* different from men. That's the point. Men and women were never created to be just like each other. It's what makes things fun, but it's also the source of a lot of problems.

What it boils down to is a communication issue. And ladies, as Strother Martin said to Paul Newman in *Cool Hand Luke*, "What we have here is a failure to communicate."

When it comes to marriage, boys and girls don't seem to get along. In the past thirty years the percentage of married men in the United States has dropped from 65.4 percent to 55.4 percent. What's the deal? Are men gun shy when it comes to marriage? Possibly. Are men commitment-phobic? Probably. But for every guy who is not married, there's a lady in the same position.

So do men not *want* to get married? Although it may look grim if you're hoping to find your Prince Charming, the truth is people are still getting married—and half of them are men. So it's not all gloom and doom. It just takes some work as men aren't lining up to the altar as easily as they once were.

"What about the benefits of marriage?" I hear you cry. Yes, married men live longer—but so do neutered dogs. And no guy is going to give up his balls to live a few extra years. He wouldn't have a reason to live. There are some things in "Man World" that aren't negotiable.

Let's take a look at some other "Man World" responses to these "advantages" of marriage:

MARRIAGE ADVANTAGE: Married men are much more financially wealthy than the average single guy—married men earn 10 to 40 percent more than single men.
"Man World" Response: Great, that's more money for her to spend.

MARRIAGE ADVANTAGE: Married couples in their fifties and sixties have around twice the net worth of divorcees, widows, or the unmarried.
"Man World" Response: Yay! All that money has been amassed for what? Grandkids.

MARRIAGE ADVANTAGE: Married men are less likely to engage in unhealthy behaviors such as drug and alcohol abuse.
"Man World" Response: Congratulations, you've just turned a party animal into a monk.

MARRIAGE ADVANTAGE: Married couples indulge in twice as much sex as single people and report greater levels of satisfaction in the area of sexual intimacy.
"Man World" Response: Sign me up! Who doesn't want that?

There we have it! The secret to men, marriage, and the universe. It's all in the presentation. Sell marriage as a product that results in men losing something they cherish and they aren't going to buy it. But if a man thinks he's getting something that others are missing out on, then he's all in. Marriage has so many stigmas attached to it that it's no wonder everyone's steering clear of it. It needs a positive spin put on it. And ladies, you're the ones to do it.

Comedian Mike Birbiglia demonstrates the difference between men and women in his stand-up comedy act when he describes a conversation with his girlfriend about what scares them. She reels off in eloquent detail her fears of growing apart, breaking up, loneliness, and eventual death. His response? "Bears."

Men aren't hard to conquer. They have some basic needs. While the Founding Fathers edited it down to "life, liberty, and the pursuit of happiness," early drafts of the Declaration of Independence included ". . . and someone who can cook a really great pot roast, who can make my toes curl in the sack, and who knows how to put a crease in my pants." Unfortunately those didn't make the final cut, but fulfilling these undeniable male rights will get him off the couch and onto one knee.

What I hope to do in this book is to give you the real lowdown on the desires of men, their needs, and how you can turn a stalwart single into a loving husband. This book isn't just for the single ladies out there with a train wreck for a love life. It doesn't matter if you're scouring the streets for a nice man you hope to call your own, you're a gal with a guy who is just branching out into the next phase of your relationship, or even a woman who has a few years of marriage under her belt. You can all learn something from what's between these pages. I hope to answer the seemingly unanswerable questions about men and their habits.

WARNING: I'm going to be honest about it—political correctness has stifled society and people no longer feel free to say what they mean. What follows is the frank truth about the desires of men, which may go against the grain at times, but it's better I tell you now so you don't end up eating a pint of ice cream and wondering why he doesn't love you.

Stereotypes of the male variety will play a strong part in this book. While no one likes stereotypes, stereotypes aren't created without foundation. These generalizations help illustrate typical problems you may encounter in your dealings with men. Now, this doesn't mean men are all cut from the same cloth. There are some good ones out there and more than you think. You may be lucky enough to own one of those special guys who don't fit into the normal pattern of male behavior and if you do, he's perfect. You don't need this book.

And what makes me such an expert? I'm a guy—and I was a guy who swore that I would never get married. I was born single and I thought I would die single, but I've been happily married for nine years going on ten to a woman who is my equal. She complements my personality and she's strong where I'm weak. So hand on heart, I'll admit I was wrong. I am better off married than single—and not because she tells me I am. I know I am.

So sit back, Dorothy, because we're taking a trip to the Emerald City so I can rip open the curtain and let you meet the wizard. (I'm betting you'll be surprised by how approachable he is . . . .)

PART I

how to find him

Girl seeks boy.

Girl doesn't know where to find boy.

Girl has to think like boy.

CHAPTER 1

what's wrong with him?

We are all products of our decisions. Where you see us in life is pretty much based on our actions. If you see a guy bumming for change, there are reasons why he got there, namely bad spreads, bad habits, and bad decisions. Conversely, if you see a guy pull up in a Bentley, there are different reasons why he ended up like that, namely good grades, good looks, and good genes. Decisions, in themselves, aren't very influential, but how people view those decisions are. You can't tell me you're not going to look at the guy bumming for change much differently than the guy cruising in his Bentley. A man's decisions are important—as is his commitment to those decisions.

His commitment will vary depending on the confidence he has in his decision. Ask a guy to walk blindfolded and he'll likely decide to stumble forward. Ask a guy to walk blindfolded through a minefield at night and he's not going to be so keen to move forward. Suddenly, doing nothing sounds like a real good idea.

So commitment tends to wane when there's an element of risk. And marriage is a risk, a *real* big risk. No guy should go walking through a minefield blindfolded—no guy should go walking through a minefield at all—but it helps if he's confident in his decision. The same goes for that minefield you like to call an aisle . . . and it's your job to make him confident in his decision.

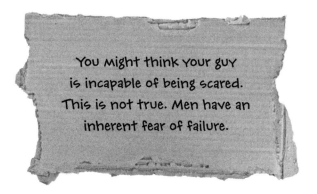

You might think your guy is incapable of being scared. This is not true. Men have an inherent fear of failure.

The Business of Commitment

In Japan, failure in business is considered a virtual sin. A businessman who leads his company to failure is guilty of a heinous crime. He's let down his employees, investors, family, and friends for making the wrong decisions, and the chances of his rebounding are virtually nil. In Europe, matters are slightly different. If a businessman fails, he is viewed in disparaging terms, considered a risk in the future, and careful consideration is given if he comes knocking on the door of big commerce again. Despite that, they'd likely be given a second chance. The United States is very different. Failure is considered a stumbling step on the road to success. What does it matter if you fell flat on your face a dozen times? There's protection from creditors; banks are forgiving; past failures don't matter as long as you get it right *eventu-*

ally. This forgiving attitude might explain the high divorce rate in the United States—it doesn't matter if a guy nixes his wife every couple of years, he can keep trying until he finds the right one.

But unlike business, marriage isn't as forgiving. There is no Chapter 11 protecting you from your creditors. Community property, alimony, and child support cut deep. And banks tend not to be too generous to those with divorce payments hanging over their head. This probably explains the rise in pre-nups. (Nothing says, "I'm not sure this is going to pan out," like a pre-nup.) However, even with the added security of a marital escape-plan, male confidence in the institution of marriage is waning.

Filing the Emotional Paperwork

Commitment insecurity is not all financially driven. There are emotional risks as well. And contrary to popular beliefs, a divorce *does* affect a man. He made a commitment to a woman and it failed. Now he's a guy who can't keep his woman. The word divorcée is hardly a badge of courage to carry around with pride. Alfred Lord Tennyson once said, "It's better to have loved and lost than never have loved at all." Well good ol' Al was wrong. Avoiding commitment does save on all the heartache. You need to assure him that heartbreak isn't in the future and that a happy end to his saying "I do" is as certain as football on Thanksgiving and a hangover on New Year's Day.

To a guy, "til death do us part" ranks up there with phrases such as "life without parole," "IRS audit," and "the cable's out." These are scary things to say to a man. Just whisper one of these into a guy's ear and watch his abs tighten. Forget Bowflex and 5-Minutes Abs. Say one of these phrases (or all of them) a few hundred times a day and you've got a workout program—you can scare him into having a washboard stomach. Ever wondered why a newly married guy's six-pack swells into a keg so quickly? It's because those five little words, "Til death do us part," no longer scare him. The commitment workout plan is over as soon as he puts the ring on your finger, and he can loosen the belt around his waist.

simon's story

Clean Up, Aisle 1

I'm no different. I remember my own wedding ceremony. I stood there, quite content for the minister to ramble through his "Dearly beloved, we're gathered here today . . ." speech, then he got to my turn to speak—all too quickly for my liking, I'll have you know—and asked the "I do" question. Panic set in. A high-speed train of questions and doubt ripped through the tunnel of my head: *You're asking me? Why me? What about her? Ask her first. I'm going to look like an idiot, if she says, "Not today," after I've said, "I do." Ladies first. I insist. Really.* "I do." *Crap! I said that out loud. I said I do. It's all over. Life is no more. I'm married. I'm so screwed.*

Things didn't get any better as the ceremony progressed. This minister, a guy I'd only met ten minutes beforehand, started issuing out this job description that went along with husband that included tasks. *Honor. Yeah, I can honor her. That's doable. Cherish. Seems like a natural thing to do under the circumstances. Obey. Well, that sort of depends on her demands. If she wants me to take out the trash, that's fine, but if it's go beat up some guy because he looked at her funny, I'm not so sure. I'm a bleeder, not a fighter. Protector. What? Bodyguard duties? I'm not sure about this one. Is anyone gunning for her that I don't know about?*

The ceremony was a very panicky moment. I was making a big commitment. A lifetime one. Until that point in my life, I'd never made such a serious decision. Buying a house, taking a new job, Sprint or Verizon were as big as it got and if I didn't like any of those decisions, I could change my mind. With marriage, changing your mind means divorce, which is messy and sad. Essentially, I didn't want to be part of a failure. But I could avoid failure if I didn't commit. If I said no, I'd be off the hook.

Damn, look at all this stress and all I had to do was state my name, repeat a few words and say I do. It's not like anyone asked me to diffuse a bomb. But it sure as hell felt like it. One wrong move and bam, the whole thing could blow up in my face.

Hopefully you can see that a lack of commitment shouldn't be confused with apathy.

He's Afraid, *Very* Afraid

Now, I may come off as a bit of a commitment-freak—and you may have a point—but I'm not alone in my freakdom. I'm not the only one who goes through this panic phase during the wedding vows. I'm seeing more men choke at the altar. One friend of mine couldn't get the words out and he'd been living with his soon-to-be wife for a decade. They even had two kids. His nine year old son saved the day by leaning forward, tugging his father's sleeve and saying, "It's 'I do', dad." Chalk this up to the side of commitment. The piddling marriage ceremony should have been a breeze, but sadly, it wasn't.

But why the phobia? Why the panic and fear?

Men fear any commitment to the fairer sex, whether it's marriage, moving in together, or dinner plans for a Thursday night. Their problem is confidence—buyer's remorse, let's call it. To guys, everything can be bought, sold, and traded without conscience, except commitment. Men are fearful of making the wrong decision. What if he's bought into you and he meets someone else tomorrow? It's the tired old scenario of boy likes girl, boy commits to girl, boy find's out girl's sister is just *way* hotter. We've all been there a million times before . . . or is that just me?

How to Handle His Fear

To break his commitment-phobia, you have to take away the risk factor. Make him confident to walk through that minefield blindfolded for you by standing on the sidelines and directing him to safety. If he's commitment-shy, it's either because you aren't the one for him or you haven't convinced him you're the one. He needs to believe without a doubt you're the one.

Prove to him that you are *it*. He needs a reason to stop looking. And you need to be it. No doubt, you have a list of needs and wants when it comes to a guy. So it shouldn't come as a shock that he has a similar list for his ideal woman. But don't think this is solely based on looks. It goes further than that. Being a total babe is one thing, but that's not going to satisfy him in every department. How many times have you read the tabloids and said, "How can so-and-so dump her? She's so hot." He probably dumped her because she was hot—and that was all she brought to the table. Hotness is great, but you have to be more than just great to look at. You're going to have to satisfy *all* of his needs and desires if you want him to commit.

To eliminate his commitment-phobia, you need to be more than a one-dimensional woman. You need to be an all-rounder. Guys keep a mental checklist as to how a future-missus stacks up against his ideal woman. Here's an inside-look as to what he's looking for:

ARE YOU MY WIFE? CHECKLIST

- ❏ Is she a looker?
- ❏ Is she a buddy?
- ❏ Is she a confidant?
- ❏ Is she a lover?
- ❏ Is she a challenge?
- ❏ Is she a cheerleader?
- ❏ Is she a defender?
- ❏ Will she care for me?
- ❏ Does she care for herself?
- ❏ Is she intelligent?
- ❏ Is she trustworthy?
- ❏ Is she trusting?
- ❏ Will she please me?
- ❏ Can I please her?
- ❏ Is she passionate?
- ❏ Is she mindful?
- ❏ Is she interesting?
- ❏ Is she independent?
- ❏ Is she co-dependent?
- ❏ Will she believe in me?
- ❏ Do I believe in her?
- ❏ Is she sexy?
- ❏ Is she funny?
- ❏ Is she confident?
- ❏ Is she the one?

It's a long, involved list, but shouldn't it be? You need to realize, you're asking a lot. You're asking for a lifetime commitment. Life is a *long* time. Guys need to have all their bases covered. Are you up for it?

Understand Where
He's Coming From . . . ?

Now you know why he's commitment-phobic and what he's looking for to ease that fear, but that's just a small step up the marriage mountain. An easy way to cause an avalanche and bring you right back to where you started is by not understanding where he's coming from.

To help combat a potential disaster let's back up a minute. If you want to get anywhere with a guy, you need to understand that men are simple creatures. Once you have a handle on that, things will get a little easier. You must realize that there are a number of little things that women do everyday that put men on edge, which puts the women on edge, which puts the men on edge . . . .

In fine *Family Feud* style, let's go to the board for the top-five things men do that drive women crazy—and not in a *"good crazy"* kind of way. And you can learn how to combat his antics without driving *him* crazy.

#1. He Won't Ask for Directions

A male's resistance to ask for directions is an ingrained quality. Men were first hunter/gatherers, combing the land directionless for sustenance. Then they became explorers and sailed the world blindly until there was nothing left to map. Now he spends his Saturdays driving around route-less in search of the new Home Depot (which is just up past the next intersection). These skills are genetic memory handed down from generation to generation.

When Mr. Man's best laid plans take a face plant, he's embarrassed not just for himself but his entire blood line going all the

10

way back to his caveman ancestor. And you being there makes it a public relations disaster. Now do you see why this is such a hard point to concede?

> **THE SOLUTION:** Buy him a GPS satellite navigation system for the car, say, "Even Magellan needed a compass to get where he was going," and leave it at that.

#2. He Still Clings on to that Ratty Old College T-shirt/Sweatshirt/Jacket

You're walking on thin ice here. College was a rite of passage for him. His life changed a lot and fast. He went from the comfort of his home with his mother at his beck and call to an independent coed living on his own with only one thing to rely on every step of the way—that college t-shirt.

It's all about sentiment. It rolled with him during every significant event those four years (or five years if he did things right). Now, he may have lost touch with his college roomies and girlfriends and the memories of those good times have grown foggy with age, but that old college T is still there to help him relive the experience. It's a buddy, a pal. You are new to the game. He's gone through more things with that T-shirt than he has with you, so don't expect him to part with it.

> **THE SOLUTION:** Tell him how young it makes him look when he wears it to work out. Compliment him into making it workout wear, and you won't have to worry about him wearing it for Sunday brunch. If you hang in there for the long haul, you too could be thought of just as affectionately as that old ratty college T.

#3. He Always Leaves the Toilet Seat Up

My answer to your complaint is, why do you always leave it down? Why can't you lift the seat after you've finished? It's a give and take thing here. Who says the seat has to be down at all times?

Also, you need to be careful what you wish for. You tell a guy to remember to put the toilet seat down and he might just do that. It'll stay down permanently—before, during, and after usage. Now that's significantly worse than leaving the seat up.

> **THE SOLUTION:** If you want to train a guy to put the seat down, use a trick my mom used on my dad. Tell him that leaving the seat and lid up let the cold into the house because the water in that bowl isn't heated. And it therefore rings up the heating bill. I don't know if there is any scientific basis for this belief, but my dad, being concerned with all things fiscal, latched onto it and the seat was always down in our house.

#4. He Doesn't Listen to Me when I'm Talking

This is all about timing and in most cases, ladies, you do pick the most inopportune times to start talking. Men tend to be goal-oriented creatures. These goals might not be all that lofty, but they're focused on them. So if he's watching the game or trying to fix an appliance that he has no talent for fixing, don't come over to strike up a conversation. He can only concentrate on one thing at a time.

If you notice a glazed look on a man's face, there's a good chance he's deep in thought. Notice I said *deep in thought* and not *having deep thoughts*. Men will tend to drift off if there's a lack of stimulus around them. For instance, the last time I was at the mall with my wife, she was talking about the shoes she had just bought and I was thinking . . .

What ever happened to Ford Grand Torinos? They were the bomb when Dave Starsky drove one in Starsky and Hutch, *but they're like baby pigeons now. You just don't see them. How can that be? They're an icon. I see a lot of crappy cars in circulation, but why no Grand Torinos?*

This train of thought will continue to rack up the miles until I'm jerked from it. This is the key to keeping him focused on you. If he is focused on something else or zoned out in trivia world, you need to shock him back into the real world.

THE SOLUTION: You need to derail his train of thought with something provocative that's going to grab his attention. Go with something like, "I was talking about threesomes with my younger sister the other day . . ." or "I missed my period the other week . . ." Jolts like this will bring him out of a coma. Remember, these provocative remarks are only supposed to shock him into consciousness. You don't have to keep the subject going. The moment you have his full attention, kill the subject dead with conversation cappers like, ". . . but she said threesomes never appealed to her," or ". . . I just had my dates wrong and I had my period on schedule. Scary, huh?" Once you have his attention, proceed with your conversation, but have a couple of shock-to-the-system remarks on hand if you see him drift out again.

#5. He Always Takes the Last of Something and Never Replaces It

This applies to soap, shampoo, toilet paper, mayonnaise, pickles, Band-Aids, Q-tips, cough drops, eggs, and any other item that he can take and leave an almost or completely empty wrapper, container, package, or box. You can see a sliver of soap floating face down in a waterlogged soap dish, a teardrop of shampoo protruding from the top of the bottle or a smear of mayo that doesn't quite coat the entire jar and you think that needs replacing. Men don't.

This is where all men see the glass as half-full—even if there's only a sip left. To him, there are a couple of more wash downs contained in that sliver of soap. He doesn't need much shampoo to wash his hair and a teardrop of Pantene will do the job. All he has to do is wrap a slice of bread around the back of his hand, shove it in the jar, spin the jar around, and—*walla*—he's ready to make his sandwich. (Why do think there's been a rise in wide-necked jars in recent years?)

THE SOLUTION: The only solution I can see is a pre-emptive strike. When something in the bathroom or fridge is getting down to the Ennie-Meenie-Miney-Mo stages and you don't want to end up as Mo, throw it out. Let him find out the hard way what a lack of common courtesy feels like, especially when that toilet paper runs out.

wrap it up

I'm sure you have plenty of your own male pet peeves to add to the list. That's fine—you should. The point of the list, and this chapter in general, is to show you that men aren't perfect and there is something wrong with them. However, with your help and understanding, the two of you can work through it.

CHAPTER 2

location, location, location

"Men are like parking spaces—the good ones are already taken and the only ones left are handicapped." This funny little one-liner sums up a single woman's search for a nice, stable guy. But it shouldn't be that hard to find a guy. Men are everywhere. They make up approximately fifty percent of the species. You're going to bump into them. The problem isn't so much finding a good one. It's finding the *right* one. You're probably asking, "How do I do that, Mr. Smarty-Know-It-All Guy?" Well, to take the vehicular analogy a step further—because cars make great analogies for men—it's easy to tell a clunker from an exotic sports model. And in the car dealership that's life, you've probably taken these guys for a test drive:

- *The Pickup Truck:* all it's interested in is getting you into the flatbed as soon as possible.
- *The Luxury Model:* is way too expensive, high maintenance, and out of your league.

- *The Bargain Lot Special:* looks like a pretty good value, but it's got a long list of previous owners.
- *The Thieves' Pick:* great looking, but gets stolen from its owner all the time.
- *The Sports Car:* a lot of money has been spent on looking that cool, and while fast, is unsatisfying.
- *The Gas-guzzler:* big, dependable, but slow and impractical in lots of situations. It has to work hard to keep up with its more efficient counterparts.
- *The Modern Classic:* pretty hot stuff twenty years ago, but fresh paint and upholstery and other cosmetic improvements are attempting to cover up its worn out parts.
- *The Convertible:* wants anyone to hop right in and take it for a drive, so when you're not around, someone else might be out in your ride.
- *The Station Wagon:* liked for its size and dependability, you didn't realize it came with passengers.
- *The Domestic:* reliable, dependable, but not particularly exciting.
- *The Foreign:* renowned for its pace and styling when compared to its domestic competitors; however, the paperwork isn't always in order and they don't operate in the same way.
- *The Utility Vehicle:* surprisingly responsive to your input, it's versatile. It performs well in all types of environments. It's fun and never breaks down—but, sadly, very hard to find. Owners rarely want to drive anything else.
- *The Lemon:* looks fine and runs good for about a week, then breaks down with some serious problems, which take a ton of time and money to fix.

I'm sure you recognize a few of these models and can probably add to this list too. However, your problem isn't deciding on a model—it's finding the one you want. A car dealership is a great place to find your next set of wheels because all the models are under one roof, but sadly, all types of guys can't be found in one location. The high-end guys hang out in one place and bargain boys hang out in another. Depending on what you're looking for, you're going to have to do some shopping around in some of the unlikeliest of places.

Where to Find Him

You have three choices when it comes to your search—your place, his place, or a neutral place. It's easy for you to look within your realm—the workplace, where you play, your circle of friends, and your family (avoiding direct bloodlines, of course). But it might be advantageous to look outside your comfort zone. Try guy-friendly hangouts, like popular sporting venues, home improvement stores, or concerts. And the third option is to try somewhere that you both are going with the intention of finding someone special, like an online dating site.

Your Place

More than likely, you come into contact with dozens of men every week thanks to your job, interests, routine, social life, and family functions. This is *your place*. This is where you could meet your man, so keep an open mind to all the men you meet. Are you looking at these guys beyond your formal association as potential partners? You should be.

I think most women look for partners in an ass-backwards way. They eliminate whole groups of society in one fell swoop. "I won't date anyone from work." "I won't date a friend's friend." "I won't date anyone from my gym." If you keep narrowing your boundaries, you'll end up with a very small pool of people to find a guy in.

That said, there are still important considerations. Keep these rules in mind when you're cruising through your place.

RULE #1: DON'T EVER SAY, "I'LL NEVER HOOK UP WITH A GUY IN A BAR."

All guys aren't just going to bars to scam on and pick up chicks. Sure, a portion of them are, but others are just there to meet up with friends and socialize. Not all guys are treating the bar you're at as a meat market; so do not immediately dismiss them. Lightning can strike anywhere. You should look at everyone as a possible date and whittle it down from there. You should eliminate a guy on an individual level—not a generalization. Don't decide to date him because you met him at a bar. Decide not to date him because he's unemployed, lives at home with his mother, and will forever be more obsessed with fantasy football than you.

RULE #2: THINK BEFORE DATING ANYONE FROM WORK.

I'd hate to rule out the workplace as a potential place for you to meet a man. Especially if it's a rule enforced by your employer. (He's your boss, not your dad—don't let him tell you who you can and cannot do business with.)

However, you should understand the risks of dating someone from the office. You're going to be under public scrutiny. You've basically become the corporate equivalent of TomKat or the Beckhams (except your dinners at Mr. Chow are actually Styrofoam cups of coffee in the kitchenette). Everyone will want to know what's happening between you two. You won't be able to hit the ladies' room without someone pressing you for a sound bite. Can you handle that? If you really like this guy and you think it can work, go for it.

Another time you have to really decide whether you want to hook up with someone from work is when the other person is your boss. You need to be very certain of his character and integrity. Is he the type of guy who is going make it personal if things don't work out? Will he fire you out of spite? Will he give you a promotion because of your relationship—or worse, deny you one? Sure, it's illegal, but you wouldn't have to sit through hours of sexual harassment training if it didn't actually happen.

And another time to pause before mixing business with pleasure is when *you're* the boss. Think about it—if you were to date one of your underlings, how are you going act? Granted in this situation, you have the power. But if things end badly, you've got much more to lose. Deleting him from your cell might be easy; deleting him from the company directory would be a whole other story.

Rule #3: Use your family connections.

A family tree is almost viral in its construction. In addition to your parents, you have uncles and aunts, brothers and sisters, cousins, nieces and nephews. They all have friends—*male* friends—*unattached* male friends. You shouldn't be afraid to tap your family tree for a possible date.

If cousin Joey is having a birthday party, take up the invite. You never know whom you could meet. However, be aware, like the job scenario, you will fall under some scrutiny. Some of it will be relatively low pressure. It will probably just be some teasing from cousin Joey about hitting it off with an old college buddy, but it could also turn into a high-pressure scenario if any family members try to play matchmaker. Either way, the pros outweigh the cons.

RULE #4: YOU'VE GOT FRIENDS—BUT BE CAREFUL.

This is the trickiest of all your social spheres to go looking for a man in. It combines the worst elements of the job and family scenarios. Any relationship you have is transparent and if it doesn't work out, someone is likely to take it personally, especially if the friend-turned-lover is a member of your close-knit circle. It's dangerous. But if you *really* like this guy and you think you stand a chance of making it, you should go for it, but know there is a chance of fallout.

A safer option is to look beyond your direct circle of friends. Just like your family tree, your friends have friends. There's a smaller chance of collateral damage from engaging in a relationship with someone who is a friend of a friend. Don't ignore these satellite friends. You're on pretty safe ground there.

The only other sticky area is dating a close friend's brother or ex-boyfriend. There's room for people to take sides if and when things go bad, and someone will lose. Boyfriend/family/friend drama takes a toll on everyone involved—and there's a good chance the losing party will end up being you if you're dating a friend's family member.

Before you jump into dating from your friend pool, you need to ask yourself: Is dating someone from this sphere worth the risk? If you're real tight with your pals, then it may not be worth ruining solid friendships for a fling. However, some friendships are fluid. If you're in that "drifting phase" all sort-of-friends go through (that time when acquaintances-turned-friends are turning back into acquaintances), maybe it *is* the best time to get close to the guy in the group you've always had your eye on—because that window of opportunity might disappear.

RULE #5: BE WARY OF DATING MARRIED MEN.

I'm not going to make any moral judgments here. I think this is an entirely personal call. Personally, *I* don't date married men. But that's just the kind of guy I am. You might feel differently. Your heart goes where your heart goes—you just need to be sure you're all on the same page.

If the relationship is on the rocks, the guy and his wife are separated, and the divorce paperwork is with a judge, so be it. That's fine. However, don't be a home-wrecker. Nobody wants to play the Angelina Jolie role. If you're the femme fatale in this three-handed game, know this: He cheated on his wife to be with you. What stops him from cheating on you the next time? Just like any good gambler, you need to know your runners and riders. If he has a history of committing then bailing by cheating, then you might want to bet on another racehorse.

RULE #6: FIND AN INTEREST FROM YOUR INTERESTS.

So, you like to kayak, hike, work out, volunteer at the pound, play golf, attend art classes, perform in a choir, or are a member of a book club. Whatever it is, you encounter guys in your leisure time who could be potential partners—well, maybe not in the book club.

This is probably the safest arena to search for a man. You get to know him through his interests. You get to see his character and you two share a similar interest, which is always good.

You have common ground to build a relationship on. And what makes this even safer territory than an already common thread is that if it all goes wrong and you can always change gyms, volunteer somewhere else, or attend a different class. Now, this may sound like a form of surrender, but it isn't. By moving on, you're not only avoiding an awkward situation, you're meeting a whole new crowd of people with more potential men.

RULE #7: LOOK TO YOUR HANGOUTS

You have a favorite nightclub, bar, coffee shop, or restaurant. And unless they are women-only establishments, you're going to find guys there too. Stop frequenting them as purely places you enjoy visiting. Instead, be on the lookout for nice guys. The next time you go to your favorite restaurant, ask to be seated at the bar. You don't know who you'll sit next to—and there's a good chance that if you have similar tastes in dining, you'll have similar tastes in other things.

Your place is packed with opportunities for meeting guys. You just have to keep an open mind and stick to the rules.

Your hangouts don't have to be purely nightspots either. Are you a dog owner? Do you find you spend a lot of time hanging out at your local dog park? Have you noticed any male dog owners doing the same thing? Use that to your advantage. It's easy to strike up a conversation with a stranger there—everyone likes to talk about their dog. Whatever your hangouts, work them to your advantage. There's a reason the two of you are at the same place.

His Place

This is where you have to get courageous. You're going to hunt for the rarely spotted nice guy in uncharted territory. This means going outside of your comfort zone and hanging out in places you don't normally frequent. Now, this isn't such a bad thing. It means you're unlikely to run into the problems of upsetting friends and family, ruining your career, or having to give up going to the gyms and clubs associated with fishing in your own pond. It avoids the issue of too much catch-and-release resulting in re-catching the same fish, which is definitely a sign to broaden your horizons.

Think of this as a liberating adventure. You're free to be yourself. No one has any preconceived notions about who you are. You can leave your inhibitions at the door. And paddling down someone else's stream means that if you make a fool of yourself throwing out your line, you can discreetly leave and never fish there again. It's a pretty risk-free environment by all accounts.

That's a sign to head for new waters.

The downside, however, is you don't have home field advantage, so you have no safe places in which to retreat. But, no one said this was going to be easy. You may want to buddy up with a friend or two for this. There's strength in numbers and they can act as your sanity check when it comes to potential targets. Be warned though: Don't bring your whole entourage. First, it insulates you from meeting the new people around you, and you end up not venturing beyond your friends. Second, it makes you unapproachable to the potential candidates you're searching for. Double whammy! The best option is to travel with just a wing lady for backup and wise counsel.

What Exactly Is *His* Territory?

Let's rule out some places that definitely *aren't* suggested. Running up and down the aisles of a Home Depot looking for a guy to fix your plumbing is going to draw the wrong attention. Don't actually go looking in strip clubs, unless you like dancing *au naturale*. And hitting the local biker or dive bar probably won't work—unless you're already one badass lady—as you'll stick out and it's too damn obvious why you've gone there. Instead, find out what kind of places your male friends, family members, and acquaintances frequent, and go there.

The concept is pretty simple. You just need to realize that guys give you clues as to where they would like to meet girls—in places where they feel safe. You just need to keep your ears open and realize when they're dropping hints.

- Your brother in Fresno is a member of a co-ed softball team and all he talks about are the lack of girls on the field. Well, if you don't mind swinging a bat, see about joining a league in your area. There's usually a nice team spirit, a low girl-to-guy ratio, and you will be able to introduce yourself to a new circle of people that probably have postgame social events perfect for meeting new people.
- One of your friends in Vegas is a serious poker player, playing local clubs and tournaments, and has always asked

you to come by for a hand. You've always dismissed it as a boys' club, ignorant to the fact that poker is a growing sport played by both sexes. It's lost that smoky backroom image and is no longer just played by barflies, guys who may or may not be connected to the mob, and dogs posing for paintings. Real people play. Real people who might really be interested in meeting you. Most card houses have free lessons and hold no-money tournaments to draw people in, so you can start slow and then ante up.

- A work acquaintance has taken up kung fu classes, and spends your lunch break talking up how awesome learning a martial art is. Think about it. Knowing some self-defense moves wouldn't go amiss, and you may meet a well-balanced man there. And if not, you're at least exercising and can take out any old romantic frustrations on anyone who has a passing resemblance to your last guy.

I'm sure your male friends, family members, and acquaintances are into a thousand different things you don't do, so look into them. Obviously, some of these activities are more guy-centric than others and more conducive to meeting men. But don't get involved in something you're not interested in. If you don't like animals, don't volunteer at the local pound. Your lack of interest will show and if you hook up with a nice guy, you'll come off as shallow and a fraud.

Make His Place Your Place

All of this information gathering will help you to construct a list of places you intend to hit. I want you to get real brave here. Maybe once a week, go to a place you don't know and where people don't know you. Maybe it's a new bar or nightclub with your wing lady. (Again, I know this can be meat market territory and you can hear the auctioneer calling out bids over the thumping bass, but not everyone hitting a nightclub is looking for a one-night stand—and you can recognize these guys from a mile off so you know how to brush them aside.) Or maybe you head out to the local major or minor league ballpark, tailgate, and catch the game. Or possibly try going to a home improvement workshop at your local hardware store.

Neutral Ground

You have your hangouts and men have theirs, but a neutral ground exists where neither you nor he venture often. So, if you're a little nervous about moving out of your comfort zone and going directly into his, these neutral grounds take the pressure off. Neither of you have home field advantage. There's no chance of loss of face or embarrassment. Also, there's no chance of offending or disappointing your family or friends.

The biggest neutral ground is online dating. I'll let you decide which dating site (and their twenty-seven dimensions of compatibility) is most effective, but will advocate it as a pretty clean and tidy way to find guys outside your comfort zone.

Beyond it being a neutral ground on which to find a potential partner, the nice thing about online dating is that the power of veto is yours. You're free to flip through e-profiles selecting and discarding at will, providing you with goddess-like powers over men. If that doesn't give you an ego boost, I don't know what will. However, there are a few things to note.

Watch out for the candidate profiles.
Sites' programs construct user profiles from the various boxes a guy will check, and sometimes they create unusual

preferences. A friend subscribes to one of the big-name online dating companies and she explained how profiles get skewed as the program's algorithm takes specific answers and tries to construct generalities. And while they usually make correct assumptions, errors can occur and something like this may pop up on your screen:

Username: Derek
Interested In: Females
Age Preference: Between 17 and 72 (but no one between the ages of 27–45)
Height Preference: 4'6" to 5'2" or 6'11" to 9'2"
Notes: Asian preferable, but not Chinese; must love dogs, but dislike cats; enjoys long walks in the rain.

Now, either Derek is a peculiar and particular dude, or the site had trouble registering his selections. Whichever the case, he's not worth pursuing (unless you fit within the set parameters), as a guy who can't take the time to make sure his profile is correct, probably doesn't pay close enough attention to anything.

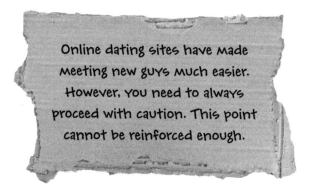

Online dating sites have made meeting new guys much easier. However, you need to always proceed with caution. This point cannot be reinforced enough.

NEVER TRUST A PHOTOGRAPH.

Obviously, people like to show their best side when it comes to their user photograph. Always be sure the user has a number of photos from a variety of angles. Also look for photographs with date stamps and take cues from the user's fashion. You're trying to avoid running into an issue like my one friend, who thought one user's vintage clothing made him look hip, only to go on the date and realize he went to the first Woodstock.

ALWAYS THINK ABOUT WHERE YOU'RE GOING TO MEET.

If you do decide to meet up with a guy you met online, I suggest you choose a well-lit and populated place for meeting your e-suitor on that all-important first date. Also, make it a place you know well. The reason for this is pretty self-explanatory— safety first, ladies.

NEVER BREAK IT OFF IN PRIVATE.

The same thing goes for letting down your online beau when you realize he isn't The One. One of my friends uses the same Italian restaurant to give her bachelor the bullet. It sounds very mafia-like when I ask about her latest e-date and she admits, "We're going Italian tonight." I can almost hear the theme from the *Godfather* playing.

Other Places of Level-Ground

While the neutral ground is somewhat contrived, it does provide you a couple of additional options for finding a mate. Beyond the online dating services, you could try your luck on a singles vacation. Travel companies now offer adventure vacations that are singles-only experiences. While the potential for a holiday romance is high, the intimate nature of these vacations can lead to more than an infatuation. Singles vacations provide a fun and exciting place to meet someone new.

Another option is a singles club. This is a local alternative to pricey vacations. Websites such as *www.singlesonthego.com* or *www.singlesevents.com* provide plenty of city-specific options to meet over drinks, take part in group excursions, or date. These tailored events take the meat market element out of meeting new singles.

---

wrap it up

I know some of these suggestions seem a little obvious, but just consider them a reinforcement of your dating knowledge. It may seem like you're endlessly trawling for guys, but any good fisherman knows you can't just throw your nets out and hope for the best. You have to focus your effort. Use the power of friends and family to refine your search. They know people and do things that you don't. Your net gets bigger the more you involve these people. The bigger the net, the bigger the catch—just make sure you don't pick up any crabs along the way.

CHAPTER 3

know who you are
and what you want

I'm very much a WYSIWYG person: *What you see is what you get.* I don't pretend to be something I'm not and I look for the same from others. I expect you're no different. You want everything you buy to be as advertised. The last thing you want to do is pick up a guy who was selling you one thing only to realize a week later that it was actually an act. Guys are the same way. Don't try to trick him into liking you. You need to make sure you advertise the *real* you. Everyone hates deception and there's a lot of it out there, usually in small print, like:

- Batteries not included.
- Objects in mirror are closer than they appear.
- Product pictured is not a true representation of actual product.

My personal pet peeve is car commercials where the ad shows a car with all the extras, but the voiceover keeps repeating base price, and avoids legal comebacks by posting a disclaimer at the end that is only visible for a blink of an eye.

The model pictured has $10,526 in optional extras.

See what I mean? You're in for a letdown when you finally realize what was in the small print. The same applies to dating and relationships.

Leave the Fairy Tale Behind

Say that you meet a guy, you feel a connection, and you want the connection to develop into something stronger. You don't want him losing interest in you and moving on, so you exaggerate a bit to keep him interested. Guys get that. It's only natural.

The problem kicks in when the exaggerations go beyond shaving a few pounds off your usual weight and using a pushup bra. Dating is tough and sometimes you have to step up your game, but keep it realistic. A minor exaggeration shouldn't develop into a full-blown lie. You want to avoid the Cinderella-syndrome. Sure she ended up with Prince Charming at the end, but do you really think the Prince bought the whole glass slipper-thing hook, line, and sinker? Think again.

fairy tale ending
_____

The Prince's Version

After the clock chimes twelve and he's left holding nothing but a glass slipper, he would have checked in with his boys to report on the night.

"Dude, did you see the hottie I was with?"

"Yeah, man. Who is she?"

"Calls herself Cinderella. She's got a real nice ride. Doesn't go anywhere without her entourage in tow. And she sports these tiny glass slippers. Where the hell do you buy glass slippers?"

"Don't know, bro. Did you get her number?"

"Nah."

"Rejected!"

"No way, man. She was in a rush. I did get one of her glass slippers though. She'll be back for that bad boy." And so after waiting around for the three-day, no-call period, the Prince figures his glass-footed beauty must've forgot where she left her shoe. So he launches a full-scale search to show off his power.

It takes him a while, but he tracks down Cinderella. Only a whole lot's changed from the night of the ball. Her carriage has turned back into a pumpkin, her entourage is a pack of rodents, and her knockout designer number is just a bunch of rags.

He knows these are just superficial things, but can't shake the fact that she lied so hardcore. He did like her, not her things. But if she lied about all that, what else is she hiding?

Despite what the fairy tale says, Prince Charming isn't going to be as easily forgiving. A recurring message throughout this book is that like Prince Charming, men are very straightforward people, who don't like being deceived. It makes them feel stupid. And regardless of what he previously thought about you, you just turned real unattractive real fast.

Now it sounds like I'm making guys out to be angels. They aren't. Just like you, when they first encounter someone who catches their eye, they're likely to exaggerate just as much, if not more. He'll tell you that he's a refuse-recycling agent, a lofty position that comes with its own vehicle, which sounds mighty cool until you find out that he collects trash for the city in one of their trucks. Similar boasts will be made about his sporting successes and his handyman capabilities.

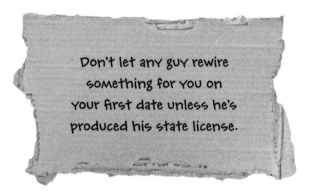

Don't let any guy rewire something for you on your first date unless he's produced his state license.

The key difference between you and him exaggerating is that you expect it. You have a heightened sense for bullshit. Your bullshit detector is NASA quality in comparison to his.

First impressions count with guys. You shouldn't come with small print that he's going to miss. This is such a key area where women shoot themselves in the foot, and it's so unnecessary. The balance of power in the world of dating belongs to women. You are always the one who can say, "Thanks, but no thanks." You hold that initial vetoing power. However, he might walk out if he finds out your first meeting happened behind a facade. So don't give him a reason to not trust you.

Be Yourself

Statistics say men lie five times more often than women. (Now ask yourself, is that true, or did I just make it up?) And despite human progress and enlightened times, we're still slaves to our genes. Males are hardwired to impress women. Watch the elaborate dances some birds go through to win over a female—puffing up their chests and using their feathers to exaggerate how big they are. Human males are no different. They're going to tell you they're richer, stronger, taller, and more important than the next guy to win your affections.

That said, our equal opportunity world has skewed the course somewhat. The days of women sitting back, waiting to be picked up aren't as common. Women can now go on the offensive. They can go on the prowl to pick up a guy if they desire. And with these turned tables, it's become more important for women to impress men.

This new need for women to become proactive when picking up guys increases the chance that you might exaggerate, or fudge certain details to land your man. Don't try to be like us, ladies. Stay true to who you are and don't let the game turn you into an ugly player.

Here are some key factors to remember:

Don't misrepresent yourself to catch him. Don't say things that aren't true. If you tell him that you're up for threesomes with another girl and you don't mean it, he's going to be mightily disappointed. Trust me, he is.

Don't pretend to be someone else. I don't understand this one and I've seen it a lot. A girl will pretend to be a hard-drinking, party girl. She'll play fast and loose and will portray herself just like Samantha from *Sex and the City*. A guy is going to latch on to this kind of personality and expect it all the time, trust me. While there's nothing wrong if that's really your personality—if it's not, you're just lying to him. No one likes to discover his sex kitten is in fact a quiet cat that likes to sleep eighteen hours a day.

Don't lead him on. As soon as he gets a whiff that you're into him, the gears in his head are going to start turning and his imagination is going to kick in. It might seem like you're being kind by playing into his advances, but in fact you're being cruel. If you're not interested, it's better to shoot him down than play up to him.

Don't say anything that is wildly untrue. Telling him that the character of Sydney Bristow from *Alias* is based on you and your counterespionage exploits is not only ridiculous, it's embarrassing. Even a minor exaggeration will get you into trouble. Saying you never diet because you're naturally thin will cause an issue when he finds your diet pills in the medicine cabinet. He won't really care that you diet to look good; he will care that you lied to him. Remember, a first encounter is the time he'll be listening most. He *will* remember later that you told him you were a beach volleyball champion with a vast collection of micro bikinis. Again, trust me.

So remember, *be yourself.* I know this sounds dumb, but it's not. If you're a quiet girl, then be a quiet girl. If you're a sassy lass, then be a sassy lass. Different men will be attracted to different kinds of women. There are men out there who prefer a quiet girl as much as there are guys who dig dangerous ladies. By not being yourself, you're not only attracting guys you won't like, but you're turning off the guys who *would* like you for being you.

Keep It Real

Feel free to fantasize about celebrity crushes, or other guys that are probably out of your league. By all means, let your heart roam free, but keep your feet on the ground. You have to stay realistic when it comes to men, as I hate to break it to you, but guys have tastes and you may have to accept you don't match them.

Let's say you're into the sales exec on the fifth floor. He's smart, funny, darts around town in a nice ride, and is hot as hell—and you think you'd make a great addition to his life. There's just one small problem: He has a thing for twenty-something bubble-headed blondes who spend their time tanning, lip-synching to Britney Spears, and undergoing cosmetic surgery. And you're brunette.

Obviously, he's wasting his time with these other girls and he'd be a lot better off with someone like you. But before you go and pick up a bottle of peroxide, some spray-on tanner, and Britney's *Greatest Hits*, you need to realize something: You're so caught up in getting his attention, you seem desperate—or even possibly psychotic. If you have to try to be his type, you're going to lose out. There's a fine line between going the extra mile and going too far, and when a guy sees you go too far, you've lost him and there's no going back. Desperate doesn't impress men.

Find the Guy Who Works for You

You just have to accept that there are guys who will turn you down, the same way you turn down guys. It's nothing personal. (Well, it sort of is, but don't let it faze you.) What you need to remember is that what you're looking for in a potential partner is someone who will complement you, the *real* you.

The Myth of the "Perfect" Man

Does this sound familiar?

- He must have a sound financial basis with a credit rating of 800 or higher.
- His job must come with a salary at least 20 percent above the national average and should include medical insurance, stock options, and a 401(k).
- He should attain a position on the board or a full partnership in the next five years.
- He should be fluent in at least two languages. If not, he should possess heraldry connecting him to a minor European principality.
- He needs to have a primary domicile in the city with a condo in the mountains.
- His vehicles need to be replaced every two years.

Is that really the type of guy you're looking for? Or that meets the mythical needs of what a man should be?

Don't get sucked into the trap of chasing the guy that will make your family happy, or will make your friends happy, or the one that *Cosmo* says is the guy every woman should be looking for this year. If this is what you want, you should stop looking for a soul mate and start a more formal interview process.

Paging Mr. Functional

Now, the world is a tricky place and we'd all like a bit of stability in our lives, if not a touch of luxury, but that has nothing to do with finding the man of your dreams. If you pick a guy for functional reasons over emotional ones, then life is going to be pretty dull. Mr. Functional need not worry. Ms. Practical is waiting for him in sensible clothes somewhere outside an insurance agency in Iowa.

There really is someone for everyone, but Mr. Functional probably isn't for you—and neither is Mr. Uninteresting-but-Stable, Mr. Still-Lives-with-His-Mother, or Mr. Not-Nice-but-Loaded. You have to find someone who is going to make *you* happy, without worrying too much about what your mother and friends will say. They aren't the ones who are dating him, you are. You have to follow your heart and not a list of requirements.

The Boy Project

Okay, there is no such thing as the perfect guy. They all have a rough edge here and there that needs polishing or a character trait that needs a little cultivating, and a good woman helps him get there. It's that nurturing gene of yours kicking in to make something better than it already was. This is a good thing. You help men become better and, as guys, we know and understand this. On behalf of all men, thank you.

This doesn't mean you can invade a guy's life and try to make wholesale changes. You can't view a guy as a pet project that you can take on and convert into the man you really want. Life doesn't work that way. You aren't going to change him. Guys are pretty rigid machines. You can make tweaks, but you can't reprogram. Your Lord of NASCAR might stop rubbing his orange, Cheetos-y fingers all over the furniture and belching up his Budweiser, but he's never going to be the super-sophisticated Prince Charming you've always idealized.

Just because you have a vision of the perfect man in your head doesn't mean you can take a guy and model him into it. If you have a vision for the man you want to be with, then find him—don't try to manufacture him.

Settling Down with He'll Do Syndrome

The flip side to taking on a Boy Project is pairing up with a man plagued by He'll Do Syndrome. In this case, you're doing the reverse of setting your sights too high. You've dispensed with any sights at all and you're willing to take the first thing with a penis and a basic command of the English language.

I get it, I guess. You've been around the block a bit. You've put yourself out there and you've been knocked back a few times.

Or, perhaps your life is so busy that you don't want to get embroiled in the difficulties of finding Mr. Right, and you're happy with going for Mr. Right Now. All you're interested in is a little companionship and someone who can unclog the toilet—but a dog and plumber can do the jobs so much better. I understand your plight, but is this situation going to make you happy? No. Don't you deserve better than that? I'm hoping you're saying yes to this one.

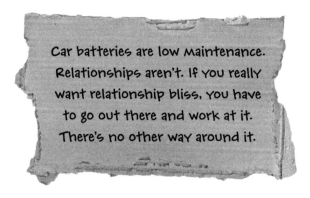

Car batteries are low maintenance. Relationships aren't. If you really want relationship bliss, you have to go out there and work at it. There's no other way around it.

Supposedly, there's a person out there for all of us. It's just that some are easier to find than others. You deserve the right guy. There is no substitute.

The Right Guy for *You*

So now you know who you don't want, and who you should avoid. And I'm sure you're looking for some magical answer as to who you do want and should pursue. Unfortunately, there is no magical answer that applies to every woman—except that the guy you pursue should be right for *you*. You are the only person who knows what you're really looking for in a man. However, any guy that you go after should have a few general requirements covered.

- ❑ He makes you smile.
- ❑ You enjoy being around him.
- ❑ He listens when you speak.
- ❑ He respects you.
- ❑ You can talk to him about anything.
- ❑ You can have a comfortable silence.

It's all then a matter of just filling in the finer details that are specific to your preferences. I don't care if he has long hair or short hair, drives a pickup or El Camino, works for a non-profit or on Wall Street. It's about what you want. I've showed you where to find him. Now go get him!

wrap it up

When it comes to finding the right guy, you have to take the Goldilocks and the Three Bears *approach. Some guys are going to be too much, some are going to be too little, and a few are going to be just right. You might have to break a few beds and eat some crappy porridge along the way, but as long as you find the right one, it doesn't matter. And now that you know your way through the woods and what it takes to find the right one, you need to learn how to keep him.*

PART II

how to attract him

Girl finds boy.

Girl likes boy.

Girl needs to feed, satisfy, and clean boy.

CHAPTER 4

food

We all know the adage: Food is the way to a man's heart. I'm pretty sure whoever said this got an "F" in biology, but I get his point. Man's need to eat has been with him since the dawn of time. This desire plays into his hunter-gatherer instinct. He who eats well is better off than he who doesn't. The ability to eat well has always been a sign of a man's prosperity, dominance, and wealth. In fact, gout—an affliction of excess—was once looked upon favorably as a sign of good living. (I think beer bellies work in a similar fashion today.)

Food also has a deep psychological effect on people. What do people do to celebrate an occasion? They eat together. Even Jesus had a blowout meal with his buddies when he knew his time was up. We eat to live. Food makes us happy. Food means we have the energy to live another day. So, food is a positive thing in our lives, but it's also a double-edged sword.

Food is also where we sink our sorrows (girls *and* guys). Hands up, who has kicked back a pint of ice cream over a bad breakup?

Ben and Jerry should come up with a heartbreak flavor . . . .

Berry Bad Breakup

Vanilla and chocolate ice cream (to illustrate the stark difference between the two of you)

A swirl of mixed berries (just like his feelings)

Crushed biscotti (to get lodged in the back of your throat, like the thought of losing another guy)

Pretzel pieces (to remind you of the salty tears of spinsters)

It would definitely be a bestseller—especially if a pack of Kleenex came attached to the carton. (Well, it's an idea anyway.) The point is that eating has a negative connotation. Food often becomes a substitute for happiness, which depresses us even more and therefore causes us to eat more and eventually the whole thing ends up with one of us being trucked on *Dr. Phil* as a 700-pound sob story. And if you think this is something only you ladies deal with, you're wrong. Guys aren't better when it comes to food and eating issues, especially when it comes to eating alone. Eating alone is just as bad as drinking alone. It doesn't look good to your peers and it doesn't feel good.

Lonely Guy Dinners

Lonely guy dinners aren't good for the soul. It's a highlight of his solo-status predicament. He's alone. He has to eat dinner alone. And dinner is still viewed as a formal event, a meal that is shared with family. So if any meal is going to be made from scratch, it's dinner. The depressive nature of the bachelor life kicks in when he eats dinner alone.

It doesn't matter if the guy is a good cook. The idea of cooking a great meal and having no one to share it with is sad, and having no one to cook for defeats the purpose of being a good cook in order to show off how great of a provider he is. So cooking up extravagant lonely guy dinners is out of the question. And if he's a bad cook, it only leaves him a couple of options.

Option #1: He can eat out. But "table for one" scenarios are the loneliest of the lonely guy dinners. There's very few places that a "table for one" doesn't really stick out. One's the local sports bar (*just catching the game while chowing down*) and the other's the local fast food joint (*just grabbing a bite before heading somewhere*)—both are still depressing.

Option #2: He can order takeout. The social embarrassment is limited as long as he doesn't eat at the same takeout place too regularly. It's a squirmy moment when the local Mexican or Chinese place knows you by sight and has your "usual" on the hotplate before you've ordered it.

This is a situation that can't be improved by the addition of another lonely guy. That's just holding up a mirror to reflect the situation. But the addition of a woman changes everything. It doesn't even matter if he doesn't live with her—the stigma of eating alone is removed. Out there is a woman with whom he eats his meals. Food is no longer a reminder of his shortcomings and loneliness. It's a celebratory, communal practice once again.

Why It's Important to Him

A big problem guys have with eating alone—besides the lack of companionship and not knowing how to cook—is the absence of the mother element. Mommy smiled when he ate his dinner. She encouraged him to eat his vegetables so he could grow up to be a big, strong boy. What caring mom still doesn't ask her grown son, "Are you eating enough?" She derived pleasure from seeing him eat well. And he enjoyed knowing that she cared.

While he's not quite Pavlov's dog here, the presence of a female figure providing food evokes a positive state of mind. Now that Mom isn't a focal point of his life, he's missing that element of reassurance and sustenance provided by a female. How do you think he's going to react to the person who takes over that role his mother previously occupied? It's going to bring him happiness. And if you're the provider, he'll associate you with that happiness. The position is up for grabs and at the moment, it's either you or the pizza-guy.

You and His Food

Just because you're helping to take care of his dietary needs doesn't necessarily mean that you're now his personal chef. However, don't frown when it's your turn to make the meal. If you're the one cooking and serving, he will identify you with his fond boyhood memories of mealtime. You're the one who smiles upon him when he eats his food. And when it's his turn to make the meal for you, he gets to revel in the role of provider. This allows him to show off his hunter-gatherer instincts and put food in front of you. This helps him feel good about himself.

But this isn't only about the providing of food. If the two of you are enjoying a meal together, his mealtime depression is removed. When it comes to eating out, he has someone to eat out with. And just by eating together, you curtail his fast food tendencies, as he no longer has the need to run down to the taco shack for a meal. Having you at his side opens up his food options. He can try places he's never eaten at or cuisines he's never sampled. He can indulge his needs and you in turn can open up his options with what you bring to the table with your tastes in food.

Know What He Likes

It doesn't matter if your guy's favorite eatery is Mickey D's or The Palm, food will have an impact on your relationship. Don't believe me? Why do you think death row inmates get a final meal of their choice before execution? Even the penal system recognizes that a good dinner means a lot. Food is a pleasure thing. It hits all the same points as sex—that's why men fall asleep satisfied after a big meal. So, understanding your man's food needs is a key element in relationship success.

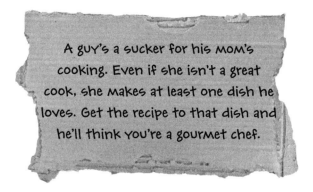

A guy's a sucker for his mom's cooking. Even if she isn't a great cook, she makes at least one dish he loves. Get the recipe to that dish and he'll think you're a gourmet chef.

If you're going to be making his meals, it's important to recognize what kind of eater your man is. Is your man a meat and potatoes kind of a guy? Does he hail from planet Vegan and has no desire to exploit or consume the creatures on this planet? Is he a bit of a fancy pants where it's wine reductions and Michelin stars that count? Or will the dude eat anything you put before him—good or bad, fancy or plain? It's important to recognize what kind of eater you're reeling in. If you put the wrong meal in front of him, he's not going to love you for it.

If you're not sure what kind of eater your man is just look at the places he likes to frequent and the food he eats. It'll become pretty obvious after a couple of meals. Test his bandwidth too. Suggest eating out at places you wouldn't commonly expect him to eat at. This way you'll know how much latitude you have when it comes to meal plans. Knowing your man's food identity is one thing. Knowing what to expect is another.

Here are some categories your man might fall in:

The Carnivore

The first thing to know is that a *lot* of animals are going to die because of him—and frequently. Cows, pigs, chickens, and turkeys are going to view him the same way Jeff Goldblum viewed the T-Rex in *Jurassic Park*.

Obviously, meat is going to be the dominating food on his plate. So know your cuts.

WHERE'S THE BEEF?

Just as Budweiser proclaims their all-American lager the King of Beers, Prime Rib has been hailed as the King of Meats. Instead of the ad telling how great the sandwich was, it gave first-hand accounts from men in the street. One such man—obviously a carnivore—pronounced prime rib as "the king of all the meats." Now, in case you've never considered the monarchy of meats, here's a quick cheat sheet to beef cuts for you:

Chuck: Where your hamburger meat typically comes from; contains collagen which melts when cooked, giving it a stronger taste

Rib: Produces the rib-eye and rib roast; can be bought with or without the bone, and has a fatty outer ring of muscle

Short loin: Home to the big boys: porterhouse, T-bone, and tenderloin; comes from the back of the cow and is the source of the top steak cuts

Sirloin: The cut that provides tips and sirloin steaks; has three levels to it: top sirloin (best), sirloin tip roast, and bottom sirloin (less tender)

Flank: Where you find flank steak and London broil; relatively tougher cut, needs to be tenderized or marinated

Short plate: A great cut for stew-meat; comes from the belly of the cow and is typically a cheap, fatty cut

Round: Houses the rump roast; a lean cut that can also be made into jerky (*mmm, jerky*)

Shank/Brisket: Supplies the meat for corned beef and beef brisket; best when cooked with the fat on top so it dissolves and makes the rest of the meat tender

Nice to know where it all comes from. Take a minute next time you're at the supermarket to look at all the different cuts and learn the difference between them. And if you're not sure which is closest to the throne of King of Meats (and you're a little shy asking someone working behind the meat counter), look at price per pound. Generally, the more the meat costs, the better its regal status.

And don't forget—weight is going to count too. The only thing that's better than a twelve-ounce piece of New York strip steak is a sixteen-ounce piece of New York strip steak. In this situation, more definitely equals happy.

ALL THE FIXINS

Now, there's nothing wrong with Mr. Carnivore. He's a pretty wholesome guy who likes the simple and tasty things in life. This makes him an easy guy to read. He's going to like his burgers, steaks, pot-roast, and barbecue. The sides that go with his carnivorous tendencies are going to be just as simple. It's going to be bold stuff like corn on the cob, potatoes (mashed, baked, roasted, au gratin), coleslaw, or macaroni and cheese. His desserts are going to be just as down to earth. Think pies, cobblers, and pound cakes.

It's easy to translate this into the kinds of breakfasts he's going to like. You're in the territory of eggs with sausage, bacon, or steak, and hash browns.

The carnivore is probably one of the easiest people to cook for. The meals are simple and the ingredients are readily available. If you're looking for menu ideas, take your cues off the menus of the places he likes to eat at. There'll be plenty to keep you busy.

Like I say, a lot of animals are going to die because of your meat eater. If that's a problem for you, you may want to sponsor a cow at a petting zoo to soothe your soul.

Your Carnivore Man's Menu Plan

Here's a sample menu for your man who likes his meat.

BREAKFAST: Eggs any style with sausage links and bacon or a meat-lover's skillet of eggs scrambled with his meats of choice, onions, peppers, and cheese. Serve with sides like hash browns, country-style potatoes, sliced tomatoes, biscuits, or toast and jam.

LUNCH: Homemade bacon cheeseburger with lettuce, tomato, and onion, or a pulled pork sandwich with BBQ sauce. Serve with sides like French fries, coleslaw, or potato salad.

DINNER: Grilled or pan-fried steak with herbed butter, or a home-style roasted whole chicken. Serve with sides like a baked potato, corn on the cob, mashed potatoes and gravy, glazed carrots, and crusty French bread.

DESSERT: Try a banana crème pie or some sweet strawberry shortcake.

The Vegetarian

Enlightened times and E. coli outbreaks have guaranteed that the term *vegetarian* doesn't instantly ignite images of hippies wearing clothes hand woven from hemp to be smoked later. Now vegetarians are viewed as almost normal. Most restaurants give consideration to these animal-friendly people the same way they have special menus for children. So good news: Your vegetarian is a mainstream nice guy. As a people, we've come so far. Rejoice.

A VEGETARIAN PEOPLE DIVIDED

The important thing to know is what kind of vegetarian you're dealing with. Unlike carnivores, vegetarians have many factions they can belong to. Just as there's different types of Americans—those of different colors and creeds, Democrats and Republicans, ones who like Chuck Norris movies and those who don't—there's different types of vegetarians:

Lacto Ovo Vegetarians—don't eat meat, fish, or poultry, but eat eggs and milk products, such as yogurt, cheese, and ice cream (at least he'll have something to eat if you ever dump him).

Lacto Vegetarians—go the extra mile by excluding eggs, along with meat, fish, and poultry. However, they will consume dairy products.

Vegans—are the hardcore boys. They don't eat any fish, meat, poultry, eggs, dairy products, or anything else that has had a passing association with an animal. That means honey's out, but maple syrup is in. A vegan diet consists of vegetables, grains, beans, nuts, fruits, and seeds. The diet tends to be high in fiber—and morals.

Macrobioticans—eat lots of grains, with some vegetables and nonprocessed protein to taste. Some people follow this diet as a philosophy of life; others follow it just to confuse the hell out of the wait staff.

Fruitarians—only eat fruits and vegetables that are actually classified as fruits, such as avocados, eggplant, zucchini and tomatoes. They also chow down on nuts and seeds.

Raw foodists—are pretty self-explanatory. All their food is served *raw* (and can only be cooked at temperatures under 115 degrees Fahrenheit).

The important thing is to know what is okay and what isn't with your vegetarian.

You also need to know the ethos behind his choice to be a vegetarian. Why did he choose this meatless path? It may be for ecological, political, religious, or medical reasons. Or it might just be to disappoint his parents. Whatever the reason, it's important to know, so that you can connect with your vegetarian.

A MEATLESS RELATIONSHIP

Cooking for a vegetarian is a relatively easy prospect nowadays, but will require a little homework. It isn't just a matter of picking the bacon out of his omelet, or replacing his hamburger with a tofu-burger. It means altering the very way you cook and plan meals to ensure that he gets all his proteins, minerals, and vitamins—without the meaty aftertaste. A great idea is including products such as beans and soy into your cooking. In addition to fruits and vegetables, these healthy ingredients pack a nutritional punch that will make up for skipping sirloin. If you're currently a little short on recipes, look to the kinds of cuisines where meat is used sparingly. Try out traditional Indian, Middle Eastern, Japanese, and Chinese menus for exciting meal ideas.

However, if you still possess a hankering for seafood or buffalo wings then I suggest you hit up the local seafood shack or wing joint when he's not around. Hooking up with a vegetarian can be rewarding. It's likely to lower your cholesterol count, but raise your blood pressure.

Your Vegetarian Man's Menu Plan

BREAKFAST: Omelet with grilled veggies and herbed cream cheese filling, or homemade buttermilk pancakes. (If he's a no-egg type, sub out the eggs with one of those egg-substitute products on the market now.) Serve with sides like hash browns, a mixed fruit cup, granola with yogurt and berries, oatmeal, or toast.

LUNCH: Grilled polenta slices with a mushroom and onion ragout, or a hearty slice of spinach and mushroom quiche (again, subbing out the eggs if necessary). Serve with sides like a green salad, onion gratin, bruschetta, or hearty bread with olive oil and balsamic vinegar for dipping.

DINNER: Eggplant parmesan, pasta primavera, or an Indian inspired feast with vegetable samosas, aloo gobi (curried potatoes and cauliflower), vegetable pakoras, lentils, vegetable curries, and rice should hit the spot.

DESSERT: Try a banana-chocolate mousse made with tofu instead of cream, or a fresh apricot-peach galette.

The Connoisseur

He's the Mr. Fancy Pants of eating. No food is off-limits, and no presentation is too exotic. He's going to know his wines and that a bouquet isn't just a bunch of flowers he forgot to get you. And he'll expect you, as his lady, to share these discriminating tastes. (Aren't *you* supposed to be the fancy one?)

Since he's all about the cool factor, the Connoisseur has the potential for being a culinary perfectionist and if you can't execute the dishes, it's going to be a long day in the kitchen. If your chef skills aren't top notch, anything you do is going to come off lacking. While it's unlikely that he's going to trash talk you for your shortcomings, he's going to be disappointed with what you produce. And even if you aim within your skill level and succeed, you're still missing the bar because the Connoisseur has more adventurous and demanding dietary expectations. So it's a write-off. If you stick to what you're good at, you'll disappoint. If you go all out, you'll lose.

Can you ever win with the Connoisseur? Possibly. There are no bones about it though, he's going to be the toughest hungry man on the block. So you'll either have to concede to eating out most nights (and learn to love ordering in French), or learn to work with him.

Can't Beat Him? Join Him

You just have to know how to work the Connoisseur. The best way is get him to play teacher to the willing apprentice. Let him play the Ben Kenobi to your Luke Skywalker. This works to your advantage in two ways. First, it shows you're interested in what makes him happy. He'll connect to this—and you. Second, it plays to his ego. How can he not love you saying, "I want to make this for you, but I don't know how, please show me?" It gives him a chance to show off his mad skills in the kitchen. You'll develop under his tutelage. It'll be a *Pygmalion* adventure for the two of you.

The key to success with the Connoisseur is to understand, appreciate, and emulate his tastes. It's quality over quantity. Ingredients must be fresh and high end, so you can toss that packet of Hamburger Helper out the window.

Your Connoisseur Man's Menu Plan

BREAKFAST: Eggs Benedict with smoked salmon, crab souf-flé, a slice of red pepper and asparagus frittata, or croissant French toast with warm peach compote. Serve with sides like buttermilk-chive biscuits, sliced melon and berries, rosemary-scented potatoes, or scones with jam.

LUNCH: Pan-seared sea scallops on a spinach salad with warm bacon vinaigrette or a three-cheese grilled panini with a bowl of homemade tomato-basil soup.

DINNER: Wild mushroom risotto paired with a nice piece of pan-seared sea bass in a coconut curry sauce. Serve with sides like fresh fava beans, steamed asparagus with lemon mayon-naise, or a salad of baby greens with a sherry vinaigrette.

DESSERT: Try apple crepes with a calvados-butter sauce, a pear and ginger sorbet, or a nice cheese course.

The Vulture

The Vulture is a garbage can on legs and is actually a fantas-tic catch for any woman. He's a Pop Tart and Hot Pockets kind of guy. He's the easiest guy to cook for. You can serve up an old boot poached in ketchup and he's going to love it just as much as a hundred dollar piece of Kobe beef. Talk about an ego boost for you.

FEEDING THE HUMAN DISPOSAL

He's going to enjoy everything you make for him. If you're short on time and you sling something together, he's going to love it. If you're a bit of a foodie in your own right and you experiment with a new dish and it doesn't quite come off right, he's going to love it. You can toss him a meal intended for the Carnivore, Vegetarian, or the Connoisseur—and he's going to love it. In times of financial flux, good and bad, it doesn't matter how much you spend on the food, he's going love it. It is impossible to lose. He likes everything.

The only downside is that you can never be sure of your own culinary skills. He just isn't interested in the quality of what he eats. Somewhere, the Vulture lost his taste buds, possibly in an industrial accident, so if you're prideful about your abilities in the kitchen, the Vulture isn't the best guy for an objective answer. But if you're not too interested in spending hours in the kitchen, the Vulture is the guy for you.

Your Vulture Man's Menu Plan

BREAKFAST: A Pop Tart or Toaster Strudel (serve hot if feeling extravagant)

LUNCH: A Hot Pocket, microwaved to perfection—and by perfection I mean heated to the point where contact burns are probable. Thanks to the variety these days, Hot Pockets come in many assorted flavors to ensure that no day is the same. (Remember there are Lean Pockets for the Vulture watching his figure.)

DINNER: Kick it up a notch from the usual TV dinner fare. Go the extra mile by putting something together from the Shake 'N Bake selection. Try ketchup as a vegetable. What works for some school districts can work for you too.

DESSERT: Break out a pack of Ding Dongs or Ho-Hos.

So that's eating with your guy. I've only named four kinds of eaters—and there are probably plenty of variations—but most guys will fall somewhere within these four types. You just need to be sure to recognize your guy's particular needs. It's important to know what kind of eater you have on your hands and how it compares to your eating habits so that you can establish a common ground where both of you can eat meals together. Do this well and you'll satisfy more than the hunger in his belly.

Too Much of a Good Thing

So now you know what he likes, but what you also have to keep in mind is what's good for him. This is where your mothering instincts are likely to kick in. Just because he likes cheesecake doesn't mean he can eat it for breakfast, lunch, and dinner. You have a responsibility here. You want to make him happy, but not at any cost. None of our four archetypal eaters are immune.

- The Carnivore is likely to have a coronary before forty.
- The Vegetarian might shrivel up if he doesn't receive the protein he needs to make up for abstaining from meat.
- The Connoisseur's diet is full of butter and creams, so he has to watch his weight, and diabetes may be in his future.
- The Vulture is just going to mutate into another life-form, if he hasn't already. So from time to time, you're going to have to say and give him what he needs.

If you want your man to live a long and healthy life, exhibit some tough love. You're going to have to disguise or hide some vegetables among the Carnivore's meals. If the Connoisseur wants some heavy French sauce one night, he has to eat a fresco the next day and go without a dessert or two that week. You may have to step on a couple of the Vegetarian's principles from time to time for his own good. And you'll just have to ban the Vulture from the freezer aisle of any major supermarket.

Now, I know what you're thinking: *Yeah, right. I'll get far in that battle.* Don't doubt your importance.

If you're in the kitchen, you hold sway. He can only eat what you decide to give him. Eating more home cooked meals ensures better calorie control and if you're health conscious, he's going to eat a healthier diet. By virtue of your presence, you change his eating habits—and for the good.

Kitchen Slave, or Kitchen Hero?

Okay, you're most likely handling *all* the kitchen duties, including cleanup. It's a chore, but let's take a closer look. You're in the kitchen providing the meals he's not used to getting—good ones. Yes, you're the cook, but you're also the hero of the hour. You've saved him from life addicted to eating out alone and scarfing TV dinners. Not only can he die a happy man, he'll be able to biodegrade because there won't be the build up of all those artificial additives in his system. In crude terms, he'll rely on you for your cooking prowess. In more refined terms, you bring a new and desirable aspect to his life. You're his special lady. Don't knock your skills and the value he will place upon them.

So, what if you can't cook? Don't worry, it happens to a lot of women. There's no need to be embarrassed. I'm sure you have other skills. No one said you had to be an all-around star. If you can't cook, and he can, you've got it cushy. But life is going to be a bit tricky if he can't cook either. If you're in the situation where neither of you can cook to save your lives, may I suggest, you learn how—together. Take a few classes. It doesn't have to be anything fancy, just some basic Home Ec. The cool thing about this is that you're doing something together and building a bond between you. It'll be a nice adventure.

What if you can cook, but you don't want to be his personal chef? It's a fair point. But digging your heels in and not offering to make any meals is mean. You'd cook for yourself, so why not for the both of you? However, kitchen skills aren't something that should be beyond him—he's not a total dufus, are you? (Don't answer that question.) What you can do is take him under your wing. Give him a few pointers in the kitchen. Teach him a few recipes. They don't have to be fancy, but it helps take the pressure off if he knows how to boil a pot of pasta, or cook a chicken breast. He'll like his new and improved abilities because he isn't so helpless, and he can help you. Again, you're endearing yourself to him through a bonding experience, while you're reducing your workload.

So part of your job description is likely to be cook, but don't turn your nose up at it. Make it work for you. Don't be a slave to the job, but don't expect to never dirty your apron.

The Exception: Men and the Barbecue

Cooking roles get turned on their head when it comes to barbecuing. Something changes in a guy when it comes to raw meat and open flame. I think it's our caveman ancestry kicking in, again. It's the nearest thing to felling some animal out in the wild and bringing it home to the tribe to demonstrate our abilities as providers. Somehow a stovetop and pilot light doesn't evoke the same passion.

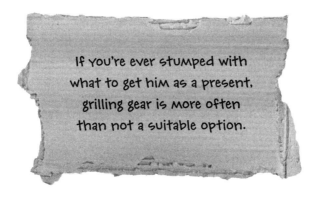

If you're ever stumped with what to get him as a present, grilling gear is more often than not a suitable option.

Barbecuing is man's work (or the fire department's, if it gets a little out of hand). Either way, give him space when it comes to barbecuing. Let him work out his inner cave boy. The only thing is to monitor his progress, especially if he sucks at all other cooking duties. Just because he *likes* the idea of roasting meat over a naked flame, doesn't mean he's *good* at it. And if he's barbecuing at a group gathering, you don't want to send people home with leftovers and salmonella. Make sure he's aware of his cooking temperature and invest in a good food thermometer. Your guests will thank you.

wrap it up

Food goes beyond nourishing our bodies on a calorific level. It nourishes our hearts and minds too. When it comes to guys and food, there are two things to remember. First, men derive companionship from eating with a woman. Second, the woman who makes his meals creates a maternal and caring bond with him. She ensures he eats well. This turns eating from a purely functional thing into a comfort thing. His need breaks down into a simple equation: Food = comfort = love. If you bring him comfort, who do you think he will love?

CHAPTER 5

sex

Sex is important—even ignoring that whole procre-ation-for-the-sake-of-our-species side of the issue. It's a source of enjoyment, release, and recreation. It also makes us unique. Besides humans, dolphins are the only other animals that do it for pleasure—and you don't want dolphins to have all the fun now, do you? You should want to have sex because it pleases both you and your partner, and increases the intimacy between the two of you.

On a purely chemical and physical level, sex is good for us. It makes guys (and girls) feel happy and con-tented. The nice side effect associated with this is that his sexual partner is going to get the blame for creat-ing this bliss. Who doesn't want to be around someone who makes them happy? And when you make him happy, he's going to want to be in a relationship with you. This is just simple relationship math.

Remember, sex isn't some magic spell that's going to keep a guy eternally enchanted. But it is an important component in a lasting relationship. So don't neglect the importance or value of sex.

Sex and Guys

Beyond the whole chemical and physical thing, sex is important to guys. It's a big ego thing. Size, regularity, stamina, repetitiveness, noise levels, and even Richter scale ratings matter to him.

If you weren't aware, there's a competition at work here—and you're the judge. Not only is he trying to give you pleasure, but he's pitting his skills against your previous partners and the skills of every one of your girlfriends and their guys. He wants to know that he satisfied you, and that the next time you dish with your girlfriends you'll say, hand on heart, it was good.

I bet you didn't know all that was going on, did you? Essentially, how well he shapes up in the sack determines how he fairs in the world. It helps to shape the confidence he has in himself, which makes him more confident to others. Successful in bed, successful in life—this may sound a little on the neurotic side, but that's guys for you.

Scoring His Sexual Performance

You need to remember that he takes pride in his performance. So be gentle in your critiques if he didn't *wow* you. Now, I'm not an advocate for ladies faking orgasms or lying about their sexual pleasure. That doesn't help. If he believes a sub-par effort makes the grade then you're not going to get anything out of it. You're always going to be dissatisfied and that's only going to lead to resentment.

The flip side to this is that guys aren't that stupid. Most know when you're faking it. Yes, we've seen *When Harry Met Sally*—but that's a movie and Meg Ryan's a good actress. Chances are, you aren't. I'm sure your guy has seen enough porno flicks to know a real "*Oh! Ah!*" from a pretend one. And don't think you don't have your tells. Your body tells the truth. Whether you like it or not, a woman's body gives off a number (yes, a *number*) of telltale signals when she's having a really good time, as opposed to just going through the motions.

Ultimately, faking it or lying only does you a disservice in the end. You might be trying to be kind, but you're being deceptive and that's no way to build a relationship. Faking it, despite being well meant, is cruel because he's going to feel ten times worse than before when he finds out. *Don't do it, ladies.* If he's not stoking your fire, talk to him about it, guide him, but don't deceive him. The best thing is to be honest, but frame the subject in a constructive way: "I like it when you do this," or "I wish you would do this." Phrases like that are going to go much further than phrases like, "Who do I have to screw to get an orgasm around here?" Sex is about honesty.

Slutty Versus Sexy

Now that you intend on having an open and honest sex life, how do you plan on getting him into the sack? Slutty and sexy are a couple of very effective tools you have at your disposal for snagging a guy. Both tactics will get you a man, but will they secure him for the long term? There are a few things you need to know about acting slutty versus acting sexy before you use them.

Slutty

It's so easy for women to be slutty. It only requires two ingredients: skimpy clothes and attitude. When it comes to clothes, it's not about what you're wearing, but how little you're wearing. It's about skirts so short that they come with a government health warning. It's about blouses and tops that are so see-through that they might as well not be there. Cut is also important, as items should either be cut high or plunge low. Underwear isn't necessarily a must, and if you're going to wear some, it should be obvious what Victoria's keeping secret. And remember, slutty dressing is a minimalist art—less is *always* better.

But a variation on the old the adage still holds true—the clothes do not make the woman. Now you may look the part, but it doesn't mean anything if there isn't the attitude to back it up. You're going to have to act like you dress. You're a loose woman. You know how to push a man's buttons (and undo them if necessary). You're transparent in your wants and desires. You say the things every guys thinks. You're self-aware. You know who you are and what you want, and you know how to get it. There's nothing you won't do or have done to you.

So slutty definitely works. Slutty will get your man hot and bothered. But slutty doesn't make him stay. And it will also get you a disappointed telephone call from your mother because word got back through the grapevine that Joanie Fitzpatrick's youngest saw you dirty dancing in the hottest club in town without any underwear.

It's true: A guy will pounce on a slutty girl. It'll give him something to high five about with his boys and be another notch in his belt of manliness. He'll like his slutty girl—but he isn't going to introduce her to Mom and he sure isn't going to show her off in front of the boss at the company picnic. A guy likes a slutty girl, but he isn't going to marry one.

Straight from the Horse's Mouth

I used to work in an all male department and we worked twelve to fifteen hour days. In that environment, guys develop a bond. They get comfortable enough to talk about anything—and honestly. It wasn't exactly the Algonquin Round Table, but it was frank and honest man talk. Eventually, we'd get around to the inevitable "chicks I would/wouldn't do" conversation. The classifications were simple. We were simple guys. The answers were: "Yeah, I'd do her" and "Nah, not a chance," but there was also a third category—"I'd do her, but I wouldn't stay with her."

"I'd do her, but I wouldn't stay with her"–kind of girls are the slutty girls. A slutty persona is good for a laugh and blowing off steam, but that's it. A guy wants more than that. Scout's honor, he does.

Sexy

Sexy is akin to slutty, but it's a different animal. Like slutty, sexy requires attitude—mainly confidence. If a guy sees that you're confident, he's attracted. For a woman to be sexy, she doesn't have to have the best figure, or be the prettiest one in the room. There's something inherently alluring about a woman who understands her sexuality and can display it without having to make a lewd remark or show tons of cleavage.

Here's the thing about slutty: It's predominately about the visual. Men are very stimulated by the visual. They're going to look, but it's a short term success. Their attention will move swiftly to the next scantily clad lady.

Here's the thing about sexy: It stimulates a guy's imagination. A sexy woman can have a guy's heart fluttering even if she's wearing an overcoat down to her ankles. The persona she's putting out there and the things she says are going to hook him and keep him hooked. A guy will want to know more about this woman. Unlike the slutty woman, where he knows what he's getting, with a sexy woman, he doesn't. He has to work at finding out about her. A sexy woman has depth and it's going to take a long time to reach those depths, so he's going to stick around.

And the Winner Is . . .

Sexy. Why does sexy beat slutty? In the long run, sexy is going to keep a guy interested, while slutty has a limited shelf life. No one wants to see a slutty, sixty-year-old woman. It's no different than the older, creepy guy at the nightclub trying to impress the young girls. However, an older sexy woman still turns heads.

There you have it—sexy verses slutty. Sexy wins hands down. Now, there's nothing wrong with slutty if you're just looking for a quick fling. If you want an actual, lasting relationship with a great guy though, slutty doesn't work. It gets real old real soon. Sexy is eternal.

Sex Compatibility

Now that you know you can hook a guy with slutty, but keep him on the line with sexy, it's time to make sure the guy you're reeling in fits your sexual appetite. Just like people are different sizes and shapes, they have varying sexual needs and desires.

Are you a sex-hungry gal? Got to have it all the time? Never satisfied? (Wow, you sound fantastic.) It's going to be problematic if your man isn't that way. If he's more of a once-a-week type of guy, the question becomes: Can you compromise? Can you curtail your needs to a couple of times a month? If not, you're going to have a problem. You might feel frustrated after a while. He might feel put upon if you keep demanding.

The same applies to your sexual tastes. Are you more conservative, whereas he's more adventurous? Maybe he's a swinger and you're not. Do you think sex perfected itself with the missionary position and this "reverse cowgirl over a rainbow" move is just showing off? Look to your differences and see how you connect. Can you make adjustments for each other? There is more to a relationship than sex, so maybe it is worth some sacrifices on both your parts to make things work, but if you two are worlds apart, then maybe you should stay that far apart.

A Sexual Compromise

Now, sexual tastes will change over time. The longer you stay with a sexual partner, the more you develop. What you liked doing at the beginning could differ two years down the line. So you should be aware of each other's needs and develop as sexual partners. But at your core, what kind of lover are you? You need to be aware of what you're willing to accept and be honest with yourself and him. You need to catalog what you want from sex and what you're willing to do to break outside of your norms. Are you willing to be more adventurous? Are you willing to change the regularity? Whatever it is, you need to be comfortable with it. If you're not, he's not the man for you.

Now, this is something that the two of you can develop over time. None of this has to be worked out on the first date. You don't have to sit him down with a sex-based word association test the first time you meet.

"Say the first thing that comes into your mind when I say the following words . . . Sex."

"Yes, please."

"Risqué."

"Doing it in the backseat of the car in the parking lot during Sunday mass."

While this would simplify life and reduce our needs for tetanus shots and penicillin, it's not going to happen. Instead, you should be listening and observing your man and comparing him to yourself. Examine the differences between the two of you and decide whether it's going to be a problem or not.

There are always going to be times when your sex clocks are going to be a little out of sync. You'll be into it when he isn't and vice versa, but if your sexual needs are totally out of whack then it's never going to work. If you can't compromise, then you can't stay together. This is one area where opposites don't necessarily attract.

Fantasy Island— Keeping Your Love Life Exciting

For those that don't remember the old television show, Fantasy Island was a vacation resort where the island's owner and proprietor—Mr. Roarke—would make every guest's dream come true, no matter what it was. Well, as long as it was legal. He never let anyone hunt and kill a unicorn, or anything cool like that. No, Mr. Roarke focused on affairs of the heart. If you always wished you could have danced with the prom king or wanted your husband to fall in love with you again, then Mr. Roarke would pull strings to make it happen.

Sadly, that was fiction. The reality is that there is no Mr. Roarke around here to grant our wishes. If we have fantasies and they're going unmet—especially if they're of the sexual variety—we have to solve them ourselves.

So why do we need fantasies? Are we bored with each other? Has the magic gone because you've seen that trick one too many times? No, it's nothing like that. As humans, we're cursed with the power of imagination. We want our passions and desires made real, but we can't rush down to the Fantasies "R" Us and get them (well, we can, but we'd probably end up on the front page of the newspapers). No, if we want our fantasies met, we have to turn to the one person who can make them come true—our partner.

Regardless of what fantasies float your sexual boat, the cool thing about indulging him is that you'll start inspiring each other. Your lovemaking should never go stale. Keep reinventing each other. One minute you're dangerous, the next soothing, and don't ask me what you'll be the time after that. You're that alluring in your unpredictability. There's a good chance your fantasies may take different shapes as you find common ground, or you find you're really into something that he digs. If your relationship is built to last, fun and fresh sex is going to be one of the major foundations that will keep you two together.

Give Him What He Wants—and then Some!

Your man seems perfectly normal, but he has plenty of fantasies bouncing around inside his head. So what could you be letting yourself in for when you ask him, "What are your fantasies?" The following represent a typical list of guy fantasies:

Stockings. I don't quite know what the mechanics are behind men's fascination with stockings, but it exists. I have it and I can't explain it. There's something about finding uncovered thigh at the top of a lady's leg that makes us very happy.

Sexy underwear. Yes, I know it's uncomfortable and it's damn expensive—for some reason the smaller it is, the higher the price—but camisoles, thongs, g-strings, low cut bras, corsets, bustiers, and garter belts are wondrous toys to a guy. Remember, it doesn't matter how uncomfortable or awkward these garments are, I can guarantee that you won't be wearing them long when he sees them.

Dress-up and role-play. Guys fantasize about unattainable women. More than likely, these fantasies have grown out of our teenage years when hormones raged and opportunities to sate our needs were nonexistent. More often than not, it'll only take a little probing to find out whom your guy's always fantasized about. Maybe it was that teacher in seventh grade, or the librarian in college, or his mom's lawyer friend who always dressed in tight business attire. These are iconic fantasies to him. So dress up and play along, but don't assume a French maid's outfit will work. Take some time to discover what gets your man going in particular.

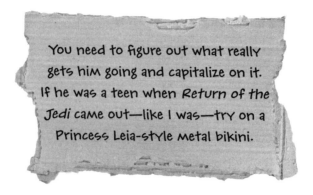

You need to figure out what really gets him going and capitalize on it. If he was a teen when *Return of the Jedi* came out—like I was—try on a Princess Leia-style metal bikini.

Dirty dancer. This is a branch of dress-up and role-play that's all its own. It's a big turn on for a guy to watch his lady put on a little show for him. You, being his lady, can go way beyond the limitations of any strip club. It's your house and your rules. Don't think derogatory—think sexy. And believe it or not, stripper fantasies also rank high on women's lists of dream sex-scenarios.

Bondage. This is where you have to really trust each other to avoid embarrassment. Some guys like to tie up their partner and/or be tied up. It's a chance for him to exhibit his dominant, or submissive side. There's something inherently sexy about handing control over to a woman or taking it from her. I'd advise baby steps here. Use things like stockings or scarves and work your way up the bondage ladder. Just avoid things that leave marks to the outside world. We all have jobs, you know.

Outdoor sex. Danger and spice and all things nice—sex out in the open has its thrill, whether it's in a desert, forest, or on a mountaintop. It doesn't matter how secluded the spot is, there's a chance you could be caught in the act. It's that danger that gives outdoor sex its buzz. It's a big wide world out there, and there's going to be somewhere fun for you to do it. Be careful, though. Public nudity can land you in court if someone objects. Danger comes with risks. Be sure you want to take them.

Three-way. There, I said it. It's pretty much every guy's number one fantasy. More than likely, it's going to involve another lady. Now if you're up for it, he'll probably think you're the greatest girlfriend in the world. But let's face it, there are some logistical and emotions problems attached to the famed *ménage à trois*. First of all, he's probably biting off more than he can chew. Secondly, figuring out who gets to touch what and where things are and aren't allowed to be put can cause a lot of issues. Plus, we all know this ain't gonna happen. It's a good example of why it's better for some fantasies to always remain fantasies. Sometimes, the realities can be disappointing.

Safety Word!

Always remember your safety word: No. Sometimes, you're going to have to stop things. Fantasies are great, but they have the potential for getting out of hand. As you endeavor to reach new and exciting levels of sexual bliss, you can lose sight of the original intent. Instead of fun being the driving force, fantasies (especially as they develop) become more task oriented—cries of "more candle wax and lucky rabbit's feet" puncture the air as you quest toward some goal. A fantasy by definition is a whim or a flight of fancy. It's a fun notion to be tried out. It doesn't matter if it doesn't quite attain the heights you hoped or isn't as physically possible as you thought. Don't let it turn into a must-win-at-all-costs grudge match. As a wise man once remarked, "the difference between eroticism and perversion is eroticism uses a feather and perversion uses the whole chicken." So if you have a chicken coop in the bedroom, you may want to dial things back a turn or two.

There have to be limits and you need to recognize them. For instance, don't let degradation become a fantasy. Always keep it respectful to both of you. If at any time you're uncomfortable, stop. Don't cross lines you don't feel comfortable crossing. I know, I know, including the Dallas Cowboys cheerleaders *seems* like a good idea on paper, but when they come tramping through your bedroom humming the theme to *Monday Night Football*, it could be a signal to reassess. The same applies to him. If you see he's not having fun, then simply stop. While it's fun to give your lovemaking the rock 'n' roll treatment, we've all seen enough episodes of *Behind the Music* to see where that kind of excess ends up.

What's Your Pleasure?

Okay, we've covered the realms of the fantastical when it comes to him. It's only fair he return the favor. If you're willing to indulge his flights of fancy, then he should be willing to indulge yours.

What are your fantasies? I'm sure you've got a couple of things tucked into your stocking tops which you've never done, but you wouldn't mind taking a crack at. Your fantasy could be as simple as your man remembering to take his socks off before climbing aboard, or as complex as requiring a permit from the city and structural steelwork being installed before anything can be attempted.

Have you told him about it? If you haven't, this is the time to do so. The great thing about a long-term relationship is that you can reach a certain level of openness with your man. You can discuss things with him that you may not be comfortable discussing with a guy you don't know as well. Tell him what you'd like to do to him. Tell him what you'd like to have done to you. I don't think you'll disappoint him and he won't have a shortage of ideas either.

Whatever your fantasies—and I'm guessing you have more than one—compile them. Classify them by fun, thrill factor, possible injury to you or him, the need for legal counsel, and so on. Then rank them.

This is important because you need to select one of your fantasies before approaching him with it, and it's important to select the right one. It need not be the least risky or the most daring of your fantasies. It just needs to be one that best suits his skill sets and comfort level. You don't want to scare him off. Ego doesn't just play a role in his fear of failing to please you— it's front and center. If you show yourself to be a far more adventurous person in bed than he is, it's going to frighten him. The person he thought he knew is proving to be someone that he may not be able to compete with. That's the tricky thing about fantasies: They're personal. But it's both of your jobs to be open and receptive to one another's.

The Fantasy Evolution

Fantasies require trust. Trust comes with time, so the fantasies you're going to indulge in on a first date are going to be a world away from those of a couple in a long-term relationship. If on a first date, the guy tells you he'd be up for a three-way with your waitress, I can pretty much guarantee that your next words are, "Check, please!" Now don't get me wrong. This may still be your answer after you've been married ten years, but at least by then, you're more open to entertaining the request.

If you're at the beginning stage of a relationship with a guy, to be honest, you don't have to go all wild and crazy with the fantasies. I'll let you into a secret here: you alone are his fantasy at this stage. There don't have to be any frills or enhancements. Pace yourself. Don't try and hit all of his and your fantasies in the first two weeks of your relationship. You'll burn out in a month (relationship-wise as well as physically), and it's not necessary. At the beginning, you naked is a pretty good fantasy to start with.

As you discover each other sexually, you'll have a better gauge on tackling each other's fantasies. Also, the initial stages of a relationship are going to establish whether you two are compatible in the first place. There's no real point going there with your fantasies if you two can't hit it off with some simple stuff.

Fantasies can be best explored when that first flush of passion has passed and the both of you are moving into a more stable relationship. There's no need to hide your thoughts from each other. You've sated your initial lust and you can talk freely about your sexuality. You can share your innermost desires now that you're with someone you can really explore with. When you've reached this level of trust, be honest with each other about your sexual desires. A couple that represses its needs isn't going to last long. Those that express themselves are in it for the long haul.

If you're in a constant state of evolution, discovering new sexual heights and refining others, then you're going to stick together.

Fantasy-Play Has Its Advantages

Fantasies can really work for you and your relationship and not just because it makes sex fun and exciting. One of the complaints women have about men is their proclivity for checking out other women in their presence. A fun and exciting sexual partner goes a long way toward dispelling that. You aren't just one woman in the sack. You're a whole harem. One night you're the dominatrix. Another you're the temptress. No matter what kind of woman he can meet in the street, you can be it. His woman is always different and always exciting. Suddenly, women in the street lose their appeal.

Keeping things interesting in the bedroom shows him that you are a sexual partner that can't be bettered. It breeds loyalty. If you know where to tickle him to make him thump his foot, then he's going to keep coming back to you for another stroke. The mindset that he develops is that he's found someone he can't do without. There's no girl out there who likes to play in the bedroom like you.

There's More to Life Than Sex, But . . .

It does make a difference. Yes, there are dreams and aspirations, callings and vocations, knowledge and understanding. Life is filled with an abundance of sights and opportunities and it's unlikely that we'll ever get to do more than just scratch at the surface. However, when it comes to relationships, sex can impact all of these things, and they all lack appeal when your love life is on the rocks.

Sex is a barometer of the way we're feeling. If we're feeling great, we consummate that feeling with a roll in the hay.

Conversely, a terrible sex life will bring you unhappiness. If the whole escapade between the sheets is dreary or dull, you're going to dread the words, "Hey, honey, how about it?" If the sex is abusive in some way, with a humiliating or derogatory component, or even worse violence, then sex becomes something to dread.

Even a lack of sex is miserable. If your partner is rejecting you or ignoring you, your esteem is taking a battering. Whatever way you slice it, unhappy in sex is unhappy in life.

Yes, there is more to life than sex, but sex is connected to life. When we're happy, we have sex and sex adds to that happiness. Sex is a relationship minefield. When things go wrong, there's going to be a lot of damage, tears shed and bodies lying face down. So sex is something you have to concentrate on. You can't assume it'll just look after itself.

At the same time, sex is great for your relationship. It creates a bond between the two of you that can't be broken. You can never just be some girl he dated once. You were his lover. Your mark is indelible. Yes, there is more to life than sex, but if you can connect with someone on a sexual level and explore a sexual relationship in the long term, there's no better way to celebrate life.

---

wrap it up

Sex is an unbelievably important part of any good relationship. And great sex is certain to help keep your man (and you) happy, satisfied, and together. You just have to remember to keep an open and honest mind to your sex life. If something is bothering you, tell him. If he's not doing something right, tell him. If you want to indulge in a lustful fantasy where he swoops in and saves you from a band of pirates and then ravages you aboard his ship, tell him! Sex is supposed to be fun, and it will be what helps you attract and keep your guy.

CHAPTER 6

laundry

Wow, here's a contentious subject if there ever was one: Who does the laundry—and the chores in general? For generations, women have been the homemakers. They made the house look good while their men were out working on the line or in the office somewhere. Times have changed. We live in a double-income world with women out there working in the same lines and offices as their men-folk. So who should be doing all the chores when you both return home? You? Him? Both of you?

It definitely depends on your relationship and the system you wish to put in place. But before a division of labor is carved, you need to know a few things about the way guys view the nature of chores. To him, there are feminine chores and there are masculine chores.

Feminine Chores	Masculine Chores
Laundry	Cleaning the gutters out
Ironing	Mowing the lawn
Mopping	Hitting something with a hammer

Naturally, he's going to gravitate to the tasks that make him look like a tough guy. These are likely to require things such as tools—especially power tools. Nothing says *manly chore* like a gas powered chainsaw, or a drill that requires 220 volts and a transformer. The reason gas powered lawn mowers sell better than their electric powered counterparts is that they make a lot of noise, require maintenance, and therefore require skills to use and maintain. Don't expect a solar powered mower ever to hit the market and sell. We can all be choking on carbon dioxide emissions but if it's not noisy or doesn't smell, he isn't going to want it. *With great power (tools) comes great manhood.* Plain and simple.

The Qualifications of a *Man Chore*

He'll want chores that demonstrate his mad skills. Tossing the clothes in the dryer and pressing a button? No skill necessary. It has nothing that separates him from other men. He needs to perform a task that shows he is capable of something that others might not be capable of. Home Depots and Lowes are filled with plenty of men who are focused less on improving their homes and more on posturing. *Me, man. Me install drywall. Me, lay tile. Me better than other man.*

Needs to Be Dangerous

Danger also plays a role in what he will or won't do. There has to be some to entice him. Now, it's unlikely he's going to pull a muscle or lose a limb from tossing the dirty clothes in the washing machine or mopping the floor. And if he does suffer an injury during the course of such chores, he won't want anyone knowing about it. Scars are medals of valor when it comes to guys. Just watch the battle of the scars scene in the movie *Jaws* for proof of this. He'll want to point out the nine inch curving slash across his forearm and say, "Yeah, that's where the chainsaw kicked back." He doesn't want to say, "Well, I thought I put the iron down safely but I guess not . . . ."

As with many things, your man has to show you and the world that he is a worthy male. Physical dangers prove that he's willing to put himself in peril for his family. You can almost hear him beating his chest and roaring at the world. This means if anyone is going to electrocute himself changing a light bulb, it's going to be him, goddamn it.

Must Require Toys

Men have a little—and in some cases *a lot*—of the little boy in them, and boys love their toys. So chores that come with toys are a big winner. Take a socket wrench set. It comes with hundreds of shiny pieces, it makes that fun clicking noise when you operate the wrench, and the pieces have to be assembled to operate it. A chainsaw makes noises, stinks, requires an intricate number of maintenance operations before it can be fired up, and it can claim a limb. A vacuum cleaner just doesn't have the same appeal (unless it's a shop vac that has enough suction to reverse time and capture World War Two bomber crews lost in the Bermuda Triangle). Tools are toys for men. They're bright and shiny. He can show them off to friends and strangers.

Needs to Be Cool

Certain chores have more of a cool factor too. Besides all the nifty tools he has to use, some of the tasks require him to get dressed up in the latest protective gear. I think this appeals to your man because of the superhero desire kicking in. He doesn't wear a tool belt and safety mask because they're practical; he wears them because they put him in the same class as Batman and Spiderman. He becomes Handyman!

Tools breed tools, as one tool is never enough. He has to have more and needs cabinets to keep them in. If you move in together, be prepared to give up some space to his mini-hardware store.

Results Must Be Evident

The same applies to anything menial. Guys like significant tangible results. He cuts down a tree and he's got the space left by the tree and a pile of chippings after he's run the tree through a chipper. He polishes the floor or dusts the mantle and he's got a shinier floor and a cleaner mantle, but it doesn't quite compare with a four foot pile of chippings. It isn't that he doesn't like polishing the floor. It's that he doesn't see a huge net gain for his efforts. Minutia doesn't really work for him. He wants big gains for big effort. I'm the poster boy for this. When I'm vacuuming, I'm not vacuuming for a cleaner home, I'm vacuuming to see how the vacuum is changing the carpet's weft and I'm getting a kick from watching the cleaner suck the cat hair off the ground. When you break it down, I'm watching for results. I'm reveling in the change I made to my home. It has nothing to do with cleanliness. Bizarre, but true.

Minor Details Need Not Apply

Dexterity is also an issue for guys. Generally, guys are broad brush people. They can sling an axe, mow a lawn, or demolish something, but they aren't too good at the fiddly stuff. Their eye for detail deserts them when it comes to cleaning the toilet bowl or the bathtub. They miss things. For whatever reason, women seem predisposed to being more careful or considerate when it comes to these types of tasks. This isn't some Neanderthal remark to insinuate that women should do the cleaning or even an excuse—it's just an observation of how men and women differ.

There you have it: *Man chores.* And you thought they just didn't want to clean up after themselves. I bet you never thought there was so much to it—or them. All of this is important to understand. As men, we aren't necessarily work-shy when it comes to chores. It's the kind of work that we're shy about. Some of it is a pride thing (we must look good in all our endeavors) and some of it is a skill thing (or lack of skill thing to be more exact).

A Woman's Role in a Man Chore World

Men don't look at women as scullery maids, per se. They just see women filling the gaps they leave behind. For proof of this, look at your average single guy. Go check out his place. He's more than likely to have a highly maintained car sitting in the garage and a scum line encircling the inside of the bathtub. To paraphrase the 80s band, Foreigner, he's been waiting for a girl like you to come into his life (and pick up after him). He's looking for someone who can improve his life—and this includes the environment he lives in.

He's going to love that someone can backfill the holes he leaves behind. Now, I can see why that's a problem. You're his girl, life partner, equal in all things, but he wants you to scrub the floors and wipe down the countertops. Who died and made him king? Before anyone gets too carried away on the rights and wrongs of chores and men's perceptions, there are some things to consider.

Your Skill Sets

What are you good at? It's an important question. Are you good at keeping the countertops sanitary? Can you iron? How about your plumbing skills? Can you change a leaking wax seal? The chimney needs re-pointing—you okay up there on the roof with a bucket of grout?

It's important to know your skills. It's a little unfair to complain about what he doesn't do, or isn't willing to do when there are things you can't do and expect him to do. So before you get embroiled in a fight over chores, please stand back for second. I urge you to employ a little bit of give and take. If you have a natural talent for some chores and he doesn't, why don't you do them? More than likely, they're going to get done better if you do them anyway.

It's understandable that you want to divide the chores down the middle. Everyone has to take a crack at everything. That sounds real good to you because you're thinking about the chores you hate doing on a regular basis. But equality goes both ways. It also means you're going to have to go up into the crawlspace from time to time and possibly wield a chainsaw. You could be signing yourself up for some chores that you never realized he does.

You need to think: What are you willing to do and where can your skills be put to use the best? If there are things you can do well, your efforts aren't going to go unappreciated. You're making a marked improvement to his quality of living and who do you do think he's going to hold responsible for that?

Certain chores appeal to the sensibilities of each gender. Think about it. You ladies have certain sensibilities that men don't possess. Yes, a guy knows his way around a washing machine, but he doesn't know when something should go in the washing machine, to the dry cleaner, or in an incinerator. His definition of clean and yours are two completely different things. If men did all the laundry, the world would be a pretty funky smelling place. The point here is that it's just not in his DNA to do a good job. His man brain just isn't fine-tuned enough to handle the challenge and no amount of education and shock therapy is going to work.

It just doesn't end with acts of cleanliness either. Grocery shopping isn't the best chore for men either. Again we run into logic issues. Send a guy out to buy a truck and he'll get a good one because he's looking for specific functions and benefits. It doesn't work with groceries. You send him out to the supermarket, even with a shopping list, and you aren't going to get what you want. The problem here is one of logic. The supermarket gives him a wealth of choice and the parameters of your shopping list are most likely not specific enough, which leaves the situation open to interpretation. Men don't do interpretation very well. You can't just say you want a dozen eggs. You have to be specific—which grade, free range, white or brown, chicken or ostrich? If you leave too many options open, you're going to be disappointed.

Like Father, Like Son

My dad was a great one for this. My mom would send him out to the supermarket with a list when she was busy. My sister and I would look at each other and groan. We knew the comedy of errors that was heading our way.

He would return from the market with half the list unfulfilled. To add insult to injury, he would have bought things he considered better. He would hybridize the shopping list. The list would call for butter and milk and he'd bring home buttermilk. He'd be suckered by the power of advertising as well. Who needs eggs, sausage, and bread, when you can have a microwavable breakfast pocket that incorporates all three?

And Dad couldn't pass up a bargain. He'd bring home a ten-pound slab of "meat." Not beef or pork—just "meat." To know exactly what it was would require a necropsy. All any of us could say for sure was it was a strange shade of grey and leaking fluids ate through the countertops. My mom would surrender at this point and throw out half his purchases, suffer through the rest, and hit the supermarket herself the next time.

Women can juggle multiple concepts at once. I think this is because of their nurturing nature. They look beyond themselves and their immediate needs. They look out for others and tomorrow. They see gradation and they aren't fazed by it and because of that they can employ restraint. This is why women can turn their minds to anything and succeed.

Obviously, there are exceptions to the rule and you don't want to lose hold of these guys. I'd suspect politicians are good at chores. They aren't just linear thinkers. It isn't just black and white for them. If they can debate the definition of "is" then I think they'll know when their jockeys should go in the hamper.

If you want a fun test, send your man out to the store with the same list on two separate occasions and I guarantee he won't come home with the same things. If he does, marry him. You've got a multidimensional thinker.

Whether you like it or not, there are chores you're better suited to than him. Even if you're not doing them for him, do them for yourself. This way they'll get done right the first time around and you're less likely to contract E. coli or have a fridge full of stuff you're never going to eat.

Those Who Can Clean, Clean; Those Who Can't Clean, Don't

Yes, he can be taught how to clean up after himself and it's important that he understand the value of this. Let's not forget this completely made up proverb: *Give a man a clean kitchen and he'll make a mess of the place after one meal. Teach a man to clean a kitchen and you'll probably have to clean up after him anyway.* Yes, he can do any job you can do, but is he going to do it the way you want it done? There seems to be little reward in having him do a poor job of something you can do twice as well in half the time. And there's no reward if you have to go over what he's done to bring it up to standard.

You can teach him over and over, but he may not get it. If he can't attain a standard you're willing to accept, is there any point in forcing the issue? You're better off doing it yourself, even if it isn't for him, but for you.

Tricking Him into Action

If you are looking to get him to share some of the burden placed on your shoulders, berating him isn't going to work. He may do what you ask of him, but he's going to resent doing it. This is no different from trying to get a kid to take his medicine. Like with so many things with guys, you need to finesse your request a little.

If you have a chore that you want him to do, incorporate equipment. I've told you about his love of toys. If removing the mildew from the shower can be done using a chemical that can eat it all away, or a device that has a horsepower rating then he'll be all over it like grime on a countertop. If toys aren't his thing, make it a challenge. Dare him into doing something. Guys are competitive creatures. He can do it if he believes he can lose at something. Bet him that you can mop the kitchen floor faster than he can vacuum the living room. You know your man. Look to what drives him to inspire him to do the chore.

The Appreciation Factor

One of the big issues when it comes to chores, for women, and their men, is the appreciation factor—or the distinct lack of it. You spend half your Saturday turning your home into a gleaming palace and he doesn't notice. You've gone out of your way to do something and he hasn't noticed. What an asshole. Your grievance is duly noted. As much as you're annoyed, barking at him doesn't help. It only serves to piss him off.

Guys take their cues from wholesale changes, not the finer details. If you build a second story addition or re-landscape the front yard, he's going to notice. If you wipe the dust off the television, he can't tell the difference. He wouldn't notice if no one touched it for a year. He'd just think every television show went for a moody, dark look.

If you want him to appreciate what you've done, show him. Don't be condescending. Just point it out in a passing manner. That way he'll start to see how things are improving. He'll be quite surprised that half the things you do needed attention.

Getting the Recognition You Deserve

If you've undertaken the task of doing all these chores that benefit him, you deserve a little appreciation. But there's a little problem here. Men are notorious for *not* recognizing good work in the home. They get used to life's benefits and forget who's responsible for doing them, but woe betide the girlfriend who fails to initiate a twenty-four-gun salute when her man remembers to take the trash out unprompted. So if your guy isn't showing some love for all the work you've taken off his shoulders and dropped on yours then you've got a couple of options.

Option #1: Strike! I don't mean throw down your tools and form a picket line (but don't rule this out as an option). I mean stop what you're doing. Let dishes stack up. Let the laundry hamper overflow. Let countertops and bathrooms go un-cleaned. Forget where the vacuum cleaner is stored. It might take time, but he'll notice when his shoes get stuck to the kitchen floor and he's run out of underwear.

When he asks what's going on, tell him. You're his girlfriend, not his housekeeper. If you are his housekeeper, you'll be providing an invoice at the end of the week for all services rendered. That's usually makes for a nice wakeup call.

Option #2: Chore Swap. A less confrontational way to go about it is by instituting a chore swap program. It works on a similar principle to the television show *Trading Spouses*—except that rather than switch partners with another couple, you switch chores with each other. He'll become suddenly aware that he doesn't perform the tasks you do as well as you. He'll be reminded there was reason he gave up doing these things before you came into his world. And the realization will be doubly sour if you can do his chores just as well as him. It shouldn't take long before you find a nice bouquet waiting for you when you're least expecting it.

But be aware that this option is a double-edged sword. You might find that he can do the job just as well, if not better than you. That creates an awkward situation where your relationship stock value takes a nosedive. So you need to be sure you're the better party before throwing down any gauntlets. You're looking to teach him a lesson, not make you obsolete.

Regardless of the method you choose, guys are prone to forgetting after a while and they need shaking up. Even if you're providing a valuable service as his girlfriend, it's hard for him to appreciate what you're doing if he doesn't realize what you're actually doing for him.

Crossing the Man Chore Boundary Line

As mentioned, some chores are inherently male. Anything requiring power tools, heavy equipment, dangerous activities, and special skills are very much man territory. However, if you're able to do something like replace an outlet, you're likely to ruffle his plumage a tad. You're making him look bad. You've shown him that he isn't necessary. The more women are empowered and compete with guys on equal footing, the more it marginalizes men. It's a changing world and guys have to change with it, but it's baby steps and you rewiring an outlet is going make baby sulk, even if he knows absolutely nothing about electricity.

Now, flexing your DIY muscles around the house will likely bring a frown to his face, but demonstrating them to the world is likely to lead to irreconcilable differences. You can probably get away with mowing the lawn with his Cub Cadet 1050 hydrostatic lawn tractor, but don't climb up on the roof to repair the shingles. He's not afraid you'll fall and break your neck. He's afraid the neighbors will see you there. He's the man. Men do manly things like fix the roof. What kind of man lets his woman fix the shingles while he sits in front of the TV? A lucky one is what some guys will think, but male pride with a kick in the pants from his ego won't allow it. You're not just showing him up to his fellow man but to the women of the world too. Other guys will view him as a traitor for letting the male side down. Women will view him as poor specimen of manhood. And all because you wanted to fix a few shingles. Look what you've gone and done now.

Use His Chauvinism to Your Advantage

If you want something done, but can't get it done, then just pick up a hammer on the way to the front door and he'll be on the job before you can say, "How do I find a stud wall?"

Men like to flex their man skills, but most times, their skills don't exceed their pride. Those man skills he told you about may not be as honed as he made out. I believe this is why a lot of home improvement projects never get finished. The important thing for him here is that he shows himself willing to perform any task without fear or trepidation. If there's a difficult or dangerous job that needs doing, he's man enough for the task. Ego and pride take the lead over actual training. The best thing is not to criticize, but offer helpful advice where necessary. Either good judgment or Darwinian precepts will intervene.

At the end of the day, if you're intending on crossing the gender barrier when it comes to chores, it's worth getting his approval.

Which Chores Are Your Chores?

I hate formality in relationships. Talk about sucking the fun out of life. There shouldn't be a summit meeting over who does what—that's why there's divorce settlements. Obviously, chores are a little different from deciding your place or his, which restaurants to go to and doggy-style or missionary, but like a lot of things in a relationship, reading between the lines determines what happens next. Deciding who does the chores is no different. Having a roster system smacks too much of the obsessive-compulsive roommate who labels all their food in the fridge, totally micromanages the house because no one can do it as well as them, then plays martyr when everyone ignores the roster.

Instead, just pick up what seems natural to you and take it from there. If you're in any doubt of what you should do, it's not hard. Guys know their weaknesses. They steer clear of anything that they can't succeed at and more importantly can't be seen succeeding at. This is why the average single guy's place resembles a dump. He's not a slob. He's just avoiding the problem.

It Takes Two, Baby

Chores are funny things. By their nature, nobody really wants to do them, but we do get some sort of satisfaction having done them. It's like voting. We are compelled to do it for democracy's sake and we rarely get what we want, but there's a sense of civic duty that we did the best we could. Good for us. This sense of achievement also shows itself in the chores you and your guy do. There are things each of you will be happy to do and gravitate toward. There are things he'll hope you'll do because frankly he doesn't want to touch them. Finally, there are things you can do together. These activities are all very distinct and individual. Just don't mix them up. He won't like it if you cross into his territory.

> Yard work is a great chore to do together. It's low stress and there are enough tasks that you can split it up, but still be doing something together. And while it's hard work, it's not particularly mentally taxing.

Chores tend to be solitary activities, but some can be done together. Gardening is one of those neutral activities that you can do together. No one's sexual identity is at stake in the yard. While you can't mow the lawn at the same time, you can work on the yard as a whole. While he mows, you can weed or while he weeds, you can fertilize. Whatever the activity, you're working together for the greater good of the yard. Because you're creating something together, it's a bonding experience. You've achieved something together. It's a symbol of your teamwork. It's also an opportunity to be together. Besides the work you have to do, the chore at hand provides you with the opportunity to chat and joke.

When it comes to working together, look to simple activities that require many hands and little skill. Look to your shared hobbies. If you sail, your boat will need maintenance in the form of painting and cleaning. If you mountain bike, chains need oiling and tires need pumping. Whatever activities you indulge in together are ripe for splitting chores.

---

wrap it up

Everyone wants their partner to carry out their fair share of the chores. Dividing the work down the middle isn't always practical. You need to make smart delegation choices that play to his and your skill sets. Divide to conquer. People possess certain skills which are better suited to certain tasks.

PART III

how to keep him

Girl is happy, so is boy.

Girl wants to spend forever and ever with boy.

Girl better show it to boy.

CHAPTER 7

make him feel special

If you want to know how to win a guy, keep him and make him yours forevermore, there's only one way—make him feel special. Now, this doesn't mean you have to throw rose petals on the ground wherever he walks or bow down every time he enters the room. (But wouldn't that be something?) No, making him feel special involves the gift of giving and appreciating. It means doing something special for your guy and reminding him that's he's the only guy for you. Call it unconditional love. It doesn't matter if it's making his favorite meal, knowing how to put that crease in his pants, or doing that thing you do with your tongue, if you don't mind doing it and it makes him happy, then why not do it?

Now I know what you're thinking, *I can't make his meals, fold his laundry, or go to bed whenever he wants because I can't be seen as his servant.* It's a fair remark. If you make him a meal, he must make you one. If you fold his laundry, he must fold yours. If you do that special something to him, he must return the favor. Nobody wants to go through life as a doormat, but expecting a relationship to be an arrangement where everything is divided down the middle is unrealistic. It goes without saying that he should do things to make you feel special too, but a relationship isn't a system for keeping a tally on who is doing what. That's hardly an arrangement for a lifelong commitment.

So how can you make your man feel special? Earlier in the book, I discussed the main ways to attract him—food, sex, and laundry—but let's take it a step further now that you're intent on keeping him.

It's the Little Things

The more you get to know someone the more you get to know what makes them happy, especially the little things. The little things are great. They usually require minimum effort, but yield maximum appreciation.

The little things can be material. If you know his favorite sporting hero, try buying a little autographed trinket or piece of memorabilia off eBay. If he's into comic books, track down a missing issue from his collection. If he misses the beer from the microbrewery in his hometown, have a case shipped to him. Whatever he's into, be aware of it and know what he'd love to have in case you come across it in your travels. You're so thoughtful. You're a keeper.

The little things can also be immaterial. Call his mom and ask for the recipe for his favorite dessert. Or attend his next dull business function so that he has someone to hang out with and doesn't have deal with small talk alone. Or how about a back-rub after he's spent all day in the yard? Physical contact really does breed kinship. It's amazing what a little hands-on action does for a guy.

You could also *do* a little thing with him. (No, not that.) If he's into animals, take him to the zoo. If he's into birds of prey, find out if there are any nesting areas close to where you live and drive him out there. If he loves mini-golf, make a Saturday of it and hit the mini-links. This is all about being aware of what would be a nice gesture or knowing what he would like just at the time it's needed.

It's hard *not* to remember a girl like you.

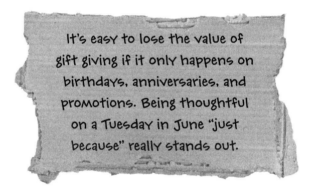

It's easy to lose the value of gift giving if it only happens on birthdays, anniversaries, and promotions. Being thoughtful on a Tuesday in June "just because" really stands out.

Be There for Him when He's Down

I've mentioned it before, but it begs repeating. A guy will bottle up his emotions and let them eat away at him. They don't like to show their weaknesses, and although they don't come out and say they're depressed or pissed off about something, their mood shows in other ways. (This is where you imagine an angry bear shuffling about the forest growling and kicking every small woodland creature that crosses his path.)

So, it should be pretty easy to tell when your guy is down. And when he is, you can do one of two things. First, you can stay out of his way and let him work everything out of his system—which isn't always the wrong option. A miserable guy won't necessarily blame you or think less of you if you don't interfere and leave him to his own devices, like kicking small woodland creatures until there are none left to kick.

The other thing you can do is get involved. Let him know you've noticed a change in mood and ask what's up. Don't approach him with accusations. Confrontation doesn't work with guys. Just recognize he has a problem and give him the opportunity to tell you all about it. This provides him with the venue to ask for your suggestions and if it's a situation where he doesn't need advice, he'll just want you to be there for him and let him know you understand and care. As much as guys rarely come looking for a shoulder to cry on, they do appreciate it. You coming to him and showing empathy feels like a cooling salve to a burn. The loneliness and crushing weight that he's been feeling is lifted. He's going to remember this kindness for a long time.

However, remember there's a time to retreat. As soon as you see the burden lift, back off. Remark how you've seen him return to his old self, but don't pester him with question after question, "Are you okay now? What about now? Are you okay?" You'll only spoil all your good work.

Go the Extra Mile

You know your man well. You check his favorite band's website and buy tickets for the next time they're in town. You hang out with him at his favorite sports bar on Saturday for college football. You go and pick up dinner rather than have it delivered because his favorite pizza place only does take-out. Whatever it is, you do it.

Now this is isn't doormat behavior or the role of the subservient housewife, these are the acts of a loving companion. A mother does everything she can to make her son happy when he's growing up. Now, he has you. Shouldn't you try to make him as happy as he can possibly be? Women tend to be nurturers. It's your skill. A man in a stable, loving relationship will live longer because there's a woman looking out for him and he's looking out for her. It's a symbiotic relationship that works to your mutual benefit, but it can only work if you do all that you can do.

Live Up to His Expectations

If you've put in the kind of effort mentioned in this book to win your guy over, then you've set a standard. He's now a guy with expectations. He likes that you understand his needs and watch out for him, but also give him freedom to do what he wants. You're close but not clingy. You don't have to ask each other certain things because you know what the other wants. You understand the value of distance and closeness and a dozen other things.

There's no longer a frantic element to your relationship—not because you've lost interest, but because you're satisfied with one another. You have a long time together ahead of you. You don't have to try to impress each other. The two of you are in a routine. You expect him to do certain things and he expects you to do certain things. This doesn't mean your relationship is dead; it just means that it is settled. Routines are natural, but kicking back and ignoring your side of the routine is completely unfair.

Kicking back is different from settling into a routine. Kicking back is when you cease to do things you normally did. You might not even be conscious you're doing this. Maybe you used to make his favorite meal, but now you prefer to microwave something out of the freezer, or serve something that comes on a stick. Maybe you used to surprise him every once in a while with a little unexpected sex romp, and now you don't bother—or worse still, you've stopped having regular sex all together. He's going to notice these changes. It sends the wrong signal to him. It tells him you either don't care or have lost interest.

This ignites a cycle that's hard to break. You kick back. He kicks back. You kick back a little more. He matches you point for point. Soon you've broken up and you're not sure how or why it happened.

Why Are You Kicking Back?

If you realize you're kicking back, ask yourself this question: Is it because you've switched to relationship cruise control, or is there something else going on?

If you've slipped into cruise control, it's likely you've just grown that accustomed to your relationship. You found him. You attracted him. Now he's yours. This is the wrong way to handle things though. In order to keep your man, you need to keep things interesting and out of cruise control. Bring some excitement into both of your lives by changing up your usual routine. It's a simple fix if you're kicking back out of comfort—just get off your ass.

However, if you're letting your relationship slide because he's not being as attentive to you as he used to be, then it's time to talk. He might not like what you have to say, but at least he'll understand your complaint. But know that if you open up the door to his faults, it'll open up the door for him to air your faults as well. This might sting at first, but now the both of you know where you stand, and can decide what you're going to do to get things back on track.

> Don't corner him. Just explain to him what's wrong. It's good to pinpoint exactly what you miss him doing. Guys don't like dealing in vague generalizations. They like the tangible. They can fix the tangible.

Obviously, the more time we spend with someone the more we get to see who they are and how they operate. Suddenly, your Prince Charming isn't the guy you want to be first in line to your throne. Whatever it is he is (or isn't) doing, it's having its effect on you. You have two choices here.

Option #1: Adjust his behavior. It's not as impossible as it sounds. Whatever changes you're trying to establish, just avoid ultimatums. That's when he'll dig in. You have to lead him gently in the direction you want him to go, or else your relationship will be lost forever.

Option #2: Break things off. If you don't think the two of you can reconcile your differences, it's better you move on before the relationship leads to marriage or kids. There's no point in coasting if you know things aren't going to work out. But if you *are* married and things get rough, you should try to make them work. You made a commitment to each other and you should do your best to stand by it. And yes, this is a guy saying this. Scary, isn't it?

---

wrap it up

It should be everyone's goal to make the person they share their life with happier. Note the word share. *Part of sharing is you doing something for him. So if you want a good relationship, make him feel special. It's not a crime; don't be ashamed of doing something above-and-beyond because you think you might be pegged as the submissive housewife. Treat him like a king, then you'll get treated like a queen. But remember, there'll always be moments when things cool down, and that's okay as long as they heat up again. If you just let your relationship get cooler and cooler, eventually it will go stone cold.*

---

CHAPTER 8

you want the ring?
go get the ring

Okay, so you have found your guy. You look and feel marvelous. You're attentive to his needs and you know how he ticks. You're great together. But now you really want to take it to the next level, whether it's moving in together or getting married. He'd be a fool not to, but he's not pulling the trigger. He's either playing bliss-fully ignorant—a very common male trait, don't con-fuse it with avoidance—or he's suffering a bad case of commitment-phobia, which is crippling his ability to go to the next stage. Either way, it's a bummer for you.

What Do *You* Want to Do?

You've got some choices here. One option is to live with the status quo. You're happy, right? Nothing's broke, so don't mess with it. Who needs racing stripes when you're doing ninety-nine in the outside lane? If this is what you want, so be it. You like the way things are going; he likes the way things are going. However, if you're just telling yourself this to *sound* happy, then there's a problem.

One way to fix this issue is to take the castaway approach: Wait until he comes to his senses or shakes off his commitment issues and drifts in to rescue you from Waiting-for-Commitment Island. Yes, it's a little passive, but miracles do happen. Also, it's an approach that doesn't impact or harm your current situation. If you've got a good thing going, the last thing you want to do is be the one who pushes too hard and torpedoes the whole thing. The major downside with this "do nothing" approach is time. You could end up waiting forever and become the source material for a country western song.

Your other option is to get aggressive. If what you want isn't being offered, then take it. Women can be hunters too. Take the fight to him. If he's the one you want, then take him down like a gazelle. *Show no mercy!* But take your cues from Xena Warrior Princess and not Alex Forrest from *Fatal Attraction*. Be powerful, not psychotic—sticking his pet rabbit in a boiling pot of water won't get you the ring.

So, you're probably wondering what the issues are that prevent your man from taking it to the next level, right? Let's review.

He's Afraid of Sharing His Space

You want to move in together, but he doesn't. Perhaps he is a commitment-phobe. Maybe, but maybe not.

Has he lived with someone before? (Have you for that matter?) It's not always as cool as it sounds when you live with someone twenty-four hours a day, seven days a week, twelve months a year. Living together means compromise, adjustments, and additional laundry. Before you even think of moving in together, try staying over at one of your places a few nights in a row, or take a vacation together. If you two can't live peacefully together for a consecutive amount of days and nights, then you might not be ready to move in with each other. A few nights together or a vacation are unlikely to derail your relationship, but it will give you an idea if you're ready for that next big step.

His Place or Yours?

One of the big questions when it comes to moving in together is, his place or yours? You probably don't realize the significance of what you're asking. Let's assume that both of you have your own places. His place is better, so you decide to move in there. If he's really attached to his place, you moving there can be seen as an invasion. You might not think you'll change anything, but just you being there can be enough. You and your possessions are going to change the harmony he has with his home.

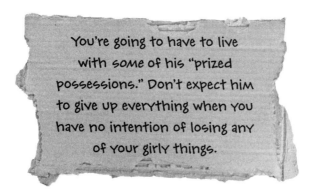

You're going to have to live with some of his "prized possessions." Don't expect him to give up everything when you have no intention of losing any of your girly things.

However, it isn't any better if you two decide that he should move into your place. Rather than him feeling like he's been invaded, he's become a refugee. He had a home with his awe-some Beer Bottles of the World collection and that car seat he converted into a lounger. Everything that made him comfort-able is gone. Now he only has two drawers and half a closet—and the beer bottles went in the recycling can.

A Home for the Two of You

So what do you do? If you want to make a home together, try making a *new* home together. If it's a problem, don't move into his place and don't move him into yours. Find a neutral place with no territory lines already drawn. This way no lines are being crossed and no one feels invaded or homeless. Both of you can carve out your communal places and your private spaces so that your individuality isn't being sidelined. Now, I realize that it's a logistical nightmare to move out of your current homes and into a brand new place (not to mention a financial strain), but who says this has to happen overnight? It's something that the both of you can work on together to achieve, and that both of you have an equal stake in.

This won't always work. You need to take into account how your guy feels about his current home. He might not want to leave it. Be it because it's the family home that he inherited, or because he has family or personal commitments that require him to remain where he is. Whatever the issue is behind why he won't move in with you, you need to get to the heart of it and address it.

Why Won't He Marry You?

Guys get a little gun-shy about marriage when they think they're losing something. Currently, your man has a very nice situation.

112

He has a good balance of friends, family, career, financial status, and hobbies. Marriage could destroy all that. Hopefully, you've known your man long enough to know all the things that are important to him. As an exercise, write them down. Then write down what will change if you two get married. Don't put "none" because there *will* be changes.

	Before Marriage	After Marriage
Friends		
Family		
Career		
Financial Status		
Hobbies		

A number of issues may present themselves in the event of your marriage. For instance, if you're in a long distance relationship, getting married will force him to leave his family, friends, job, and home behind. That's quite the upheaval, and a decision not to be taken lightly. Will getting married put an additional financial burden on him? Will he have to support you? Will your bills be doubled and not halved? Money problems are a bigger home wrecker than infidelity. Where do you stand when it comes to his hobbies? Are you okay with his skydiving or amateur boxing? Are these things you expect him to drop when you tie the knot? What kind of relationship do you have with your in-laws to be? If it's bumpy now, it's probably not going to improve if you get married. This is going to be a concern on his mind. Your man is going to come with his entourage of buddies. What are they like? Do you like them? Will he stop seeing them?

Be Honest with Him, and Yourself

You'll see that these issues are as important for you to answer as him. The point of this exercise is that when you discuss the topic of marriage with him you can give him assurances and dispel misconceptions. When you say its okay for him to hang with his friends, you have to mean it. When he asks you about seeing his parents once a week and you say yes, you have to mean it. When you tell him it's not a problem that he goes golfing every other Saturday, *you have to mean it*. You've thought it through and you can live with the consequences. If you give him a vague answer, or one you don't mean, he'll be able to tell, and that's going to reinforce his fears about not getting married. At the end of the day, you need to be honest with yourself and him if you think marriage is in your future.

Getting to the Aisle

You want to get married—does he know that? That might seem like a crazy question, but it isn't. There you are, set on getting married and you're dead sure he's going to pop the question because you've seen him sitting, looking wistful, deep in thought. But how sure are you that he's dreaming about walking down the aisle, and not the new flavor of Doritos hitting stores next week.

I'll say this again for the hard of hearing: Guys are terrible mind readers. If your relationship is going at a nice pace, he's not going to change that. Why mess with a good thing? If you want to get married, you have to bring the subject up with him.

Hopefully, these tactics will help you get the point across:

Tactic #1: Do It

If there's something you want to happen, make it happen. You do this in every other aspect of your life. You want a new job, you get one. You want a new car, you buy one. You want to drink six tequila shots while wearing a sombrero on Friday night, you do it. But when it comes to your relationship, you leave it up to someone else. (And here I thought you were an independent, forward thinking, twenty-first century woman.) It's time for you to saddle up and take charge.

If you want to get married, tell him. This isn't a Gothic romance novel. Sitting idly by, pining away, isn't going to get a ring on your finger. The silent treatment doesn't work with guys. They need the information broadcast to them in HD. To him, your silence means everything is cool. If you want something from him, *you* have to ask for it.

But Remember . . .

Your new confidence aside, the timing has to be correct. If you're going to hit him with a big question, you have to pick your time and place carefully. You're asking him about a big decision. Hit him with it at the wrong time and it will all go sideways. You could scare him and never see him again.

Do you think a guy just springs the big question on a girl out of the blue? No, he doesn't. Weeks of obsessing and planning go on before he pops the Big One. Don't think it's a coincidence he's taken you to your favorite restaurant and your family just happens to be waiting in the wings. It's the product of meticulous planning and execution. (Shocking, I know.)

If *you're* planning to ask *him* to make such an important decision about your relationship, you too need to think it all through. You need to have a plan that is a cross between a hostage exchange and an act of seduction.

How to Pop the Big One

1. Remember, no sudden movements. You don't want to frighten him. So don't hit him with the big question in the middle of breakfast.

2. You want him relaxed and you want his full attention. This means no asking him while he's distracted, like during the Super Bowl (not even halftime), or when he's holding sharp implements. You want to select a stable time in his life. There's no point in raising life changing questions when he's in the middle of an IRS audit. He needs to be at peace with the world. It's a great place made better with you in it. You want him passive with his mind idling so it's open to new ideas and concepts.

3. It needs to happen on neutral ground. If you spring this on him at your parents' house or a big social gathering where there will be witnesses, it's going to feel like a trap. He'll want to bolt for safety. This is a private moment and it needs to be dealt with privately. If you want to load the dice in your favor, make the neutral ground somewhere he's familiar with and likes. Take him to

one of his favorite places. Take him to somewhere he doesn't know and it's going to feel like an exit episode for a character from the *Sopranos*.

4. Don't dress up what you're asking for in fluff and fancy wrappings. Play it straight. State the facts, your needs, and feelings. It may sound business-like, but it's a language he understands. You start muddying the waters by encasing your demand in some elaborate story that is left open to interpretation and you've lost him. He won't know if you're trying to leave him, marry him, inform him of a fatal disease, or give him the recipe for goulash. Guys like things in black and white. Save the extravagance for the centerpieces at your wedding.

5. Know if your man is a flight risk. Is he ready for you to hit him with this big decision? Some guys are commitment shy. What a shocker! You can do everything right and still be wrong. You ask him about marriage and that could be the last you see of him. So be aware of your man. Is your guy the kind of guy to have a safe deposit box somewhere with cash, a change of clothes, a plane ticket out of state, and a new identity? If he is like this, you'll have to play it very conservative with him. This doesn't mean do nothing and hope that he'll come around one day. No, you'll just have to take a slightly different approach with him. Instead of hitting him with the big question, ease him into the subject with a series of decisions for him to make over time. Immerse him in the idea the same way you get into an overheated bath—one sensitive bit at a time. If commitment scares the crap out of him, you're going to want to handle him with kid gloves, while still getting what you want.

Yes, I know all this sounds very manipulative and it is in a way, but you're ladies and you're good at this sort of thing, so you're bound to succeed.

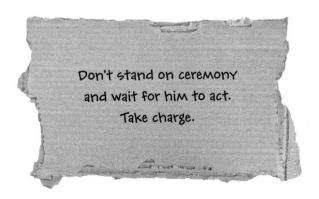

Don't stand on ceremony and wait for him to act. Take charge.

Tactic #2: Use His Mom to Your Advantage

Sometimes, your efforts alone aren't enough. Your direct approach hasn't worked with him, so maybe it's time to bring out the big guns—his mom.

Assuming you both have a good relationship with his mom, she can be a useful ally. Just approach her and let her know how you feel and be honest about it. Moms pick up on any underhanded intentions or motives. Confide in her. Let her be your confidant. Tell her your hopes and dreams with her son. All a mom wants is for her son to be happy and if you're filling her head with the realities of that dream, she's going to be on board.

Once you have her on your side, you can begin a campaign that strikes him on two fronts. On one front, you're gearing up to ask him to make the big decision with a series of what-if scenarios about your future. On the other front, his mom is battering him with "what a fool he is if he lets this girl get away"-type remarks. His mom, being his mom, can be more direct than you can ever be. She really can go for his jugular without any negative consequences.

Don't be afraid to call in allies to the battle. If his mom isn't a candidate, then find another close female relative or friend. If she agrees with your point of view and has influence over him, she will help sway him into the marriage frame of mind.

Tactic #3: Remind Him What He'd Be Missing

This is where you can really show him what he'd be missing. Scare him a little by reinforcing the fact that you're not entirely off the market, and that there are consequences to him not making you his one and only woman.

If some guy checked you out at work that day or on the street during lunch, let him know. Tell him how you hit the clubs with your girlfriends and three guys asked you out on dates. Just lay down the facts. Don't inflame the situation with some sort of put down along the lines of, "See what happens when men see me? They want me. If you don't do something about it, then I might stop turning these guys down." Being explicit isn't needed. His mind has already gone there. He'll see the potential folly of his ways if he doesn't do something soon.

What you're doing here is highlighting the fact that he can't take you for granted, and that if he doesn't shape up his act, he's going to lose you.

Tactic #4: Give Him an Ultimatum

Going on the offensive with an ultimatum means that you know what you want and it's either take it, or leave it. This isn't just *asking* him about marriage. It's saying you're either getting married, or you're getting out.

While this is a strong approach, you must make sure it doesn't seem like you're backing him into a corner. It won't work in your favor. It's just going to ignite his male pride, causing him to dig his heels in, and opt for the spiteful answer. So if you make it sound like a forceful "take it or leave it," he's likely to leave it.

The important thing is to be straightforward and honest, while being soft and caring. You need to make him realize that your mind is made up, and it's time for him to make his own decision. As long as he feels he's being given a chance to decide—rather than pressured into one way or the other—he should make a sincere choice. The only downside is that you have to live with that choice if it's "no."

---

wrap it up

Getting a man to commit is not an easy thing to do. However, you've spent enough time finding and attracting him that getting him to settle down shouldn't be a problem. You just need to have a well thought-out plan, and be ready for the consequences of your actions. As long as you are honest, getting your man to commit should be as easy as keeping him satisfied.

CHAPTER 9

keep the spark alive

You can almost hear a man's soul wither and die when he comes to the realization that he's committed himself to having sex with the same woman for the rest of his life. (Okay, so that's a little over-the-top, but you get the gist.) He's no longer a free agent able to gallivant among the unattached women of the world. Women will never look at him in the same way because he's attached. Guys will exclude him from activities because he's "the married guy." The fear of sex with the same woman comes from the fact that he's lost his bachelor-status—not that you're a poor lay. Your job is to ease that fear by showing him the advantages of monogamous sex.

simon's story

Spice It Up

A single guy recently got on my back about being married. His point was as a single man, he's free to sample from a wide menu of females whenever he wants, whereas I, the married guy, am stuck with chicken every night. This assessment is not without value. My single buddy is right. He *does* have a variety of options. However, it's been some time since he's dined out. One of the interesting stats I quoted at the beginning of the book is that married guys and guys in relationships have sex more often than their unattached counterparts. So while he does have a lot to choose from, he's likely to be eating alone.

And yes, his remark about chicken dinners is true, but I've always been partial to chicken. Chicken might be the only item on the menu, but there are lots of recipes for chicken. The key is in the spices you use.

Lose the Routine, but Keep the Regularity

Guys are scared of sex with the same person because it becomes routine. There's always the first flush of excitement when you get someone into bed. You don't know what they're going to be like. They don't know what you're going to be like. It might be crap. It might be fantastic. It doesn't matter because there's the thrill of discovery. The same isn't true for routine sex.

Once a guy commits to a relationship, that excitement associated with sex with a new person is lost. There's no new fancy wrapping to remove. There's no previously unseen toy in the box. There's just you and he's seen it all before. When routine takes a grip, he's also done it all before. If your rolls in the hay always take place at the same time and in the same place—like in the bedroom after *CSI*—then routine has set in. You've become that chicken dinner. You're a bargain bucket of KFC, two thighs and two breasts, complete with coleslaw and a napkin in case of spills. I'm sure he likes KFC, but no one wants it every day.

Obviously, routine has to be eliminated and not just for the sake of routine. The elimination of routine removes that feeling of being trapped. But don't let the loss of routine translate into a lack of sex. Just because you shouldn't be doing it every night at the same time in the same place, doesn't mean you shouldn't be doing it every night. It's adding spontaneity and variety that eliminates routine.

If routine is eliminated, the excitement remains. Yes, he might know who he's unwrapping, but he doesn't know when or where or what he's getting. You want to shake things up to prevent routine from setting in. How do you do that? Well, here's a number of options.

Option #1: Forget the Schedule

If friends can set their watches by your lovemaking, then you're working on a schedule. And the word *schedule* shouldn't be part of your sex life. Nobody ever said you can only have sex at night. You can do it any time you want—in the morning before work, during a lunchtime tryst, between dinner courses, or during reruns of *Seinfeld*. Just remember, there are no rules. Just roll with your hormones. If the fancy strikes you and it isn't totally inappropriate, any time is a good time for sexy fun time.

Option #2: The Quickie

I think the quickie gets a lot of bad press. The brevity associated with the quickie means it can be misconstrued that he's a sprinter and not a marathoner, but it shouldn't be looked upon in that sense. A quickie is perfect if you don't have the time for something more elaborate. It's something impromptu and unexpected. It's a quick piece of fun to be had. The cool thing about the quickie is that it can happen at the drop of a hat and he has no idea when it could strike. It'll keep him on his toes.

Option #3: Return to Old Haunts

As the two of you become more accustomed to each other, it's easy to forget how you first hooked up. Do you remember that flush of excitement when you got him into bed for the first time? When and where did you and he first get it on? Was it somewhere special or in the back of his car? What were the circumstances leading up to it? While living in the past smacks of desperation, there's nothing to say you can't go back in time every now and again. There had to be something special about those times that gave you two a buzz. Focus on those elements and explore. If you loved the feeling of making love outside or in the back of car, there's no reason you can't again.

Option #4: Stay Curious

You know his body. You know his sexual likes and dislikes. And he knows the same about you. There's nothing new to learn. Right?

Wrong. (At least I hope.) People change. Their tastes change. This means you can rediscover him all over again from "Oh, no, no, no, stop that," to "Oh, my God, don't stop."

Don't take him for granted on a sexual level. There may be reasons why you and he steer away from certain sexual things. Maybe he doesn't like to be touched a certain way because a previous partner always did it wrong. That doesn't mean you can't do it right. You two are in it for the long haul, so you have some time on your hands. There will be plenty of opportunities to get it right. Let him be your guide.

The same applies to what you already do well. Just because you know how to ring his bell, doesn't mean you can't strike it with a different clapper. You can always improve. This is the time to refine your skills.

Option #5: Get Playful

Surprise him by coming home provocatively dressed and ask to be punished for being bad. Make dinner for him where you're the only ingredient. Incorporate games by putting erotic spins on classics like Chutes and Ladders and Twister. Or invent your own game for sexual pleasure. How about a game where if one of you taps the other on the shoulder, you have to drop whatever you're doing and do whatever your partner requests.

Option #6: Get Some Outside Influences

Check out what materials exist out there. The *Kama Sutra* has been around for quite awhile for a reason. It might be worth a look. And there are enough DVDs out there to scare Hugh Hefner. It might be fun to check out the odd title or three.

Where the Wild Things Are

(This is your bedroom, in case you were wondering.) While it's fun and exciting to spice things up in the backyard, across the dining room table or in a national park, you can get only get away with so much before it becomes too public or ruins the antique pine finish. So even though you've ventured outside of the bedroom, some things are better off left inside.

Turn your bedroom into the nerve center for all things hot and heavy. Whatever you're into or whatever you'd like to try, make your bedroom the one place where you can literally leave your inhibitions at the door.

Mind the Furnishings—and the Neighbors

If you do turn your bedroom into a boudoir, there are a couple of things to take into consideration.

1. Make sure you have somewhere secure to hang some of those sexy outfits and for keeping toys, oils, nonperishable food stuffs, handcuffs (remember to keeps the keys in an easy to reach place), and the like.
2. If you're planning to create a category-5 hurricane in your bedroom, take precautions not to harm innocent bystanders—such as your neighbors. Make sure no one can see into your bedroom. Pull the drapes, unless you have a bit of an exhibitionist bent. And don't forget the noise levels. If you're a loud one, then flick on the TV, maybe ESPN or some other sports channel. A roaring stadium will give you the impression that you have thousands of adoring fans cheering you on. Go team!

This may sound like you're doing a lot of the work, but you're not. You're sending your man a message. You're telling him that you may be one woman, but you've got one hell of a set of skills. And while there may be a thousand ladies out there waiting for a man just like him to fly them to the moon, it doesn't matter. His dance card is already full. He's got you.

Your man just needs reassurance that he isn't getting the same chicken dinner every night. Once he latches onto the fact that he has one great ingredient that can run the gambit of flavors from mild to red hot spicy, he's not going to be interested in what's on any other menu.

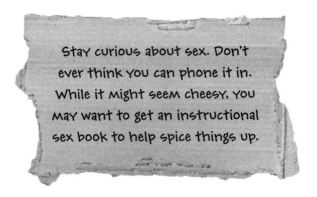

Stay curious about sex. Don't ever think you can phone it in. While it might seem cheesy, you may want to get an instructional sex book to help spice things up.

Paging Dr. Ruth

Whatever you do, you want to keep your sex life healthy. If the sex is bad, then the relationship is bad and he's more likely to cheat when he's unhappy. If he's sexually satisfied, he isn't going to search elsewhere for it. A happy dog is a good dog. Sex is a safety blanket for men. It reaffirms their belief in themselves. Despite what's happening in his life, he's still got the magic between the sheets.

If things have gone a little stale in the bedroom or downright frosty, then may I suggest a couple of strategies?

Communicate with Him

Communication is a woman's strongest skill, so use it. Find out what the problem is. But again, *don't be confrontational about it*. If you broadside him with accusations about his lack of attention or interest, he's going to go on the defensive. And don't attack his poor performance in bed. You're drawing a line in the dirt that can't be erased.

You have to be specific, but don't try to guess at what he's feeling. You may have an idea, but you don't know, so don't try. Stick to you. Your needs and feelings are the only ones you can be certain about, so talk about those. Tell him what you miss, what you've noticed, and ask if he's noticed the same thing. If he plays a little dumb, give examples that support your argument, such as lack of passion or the drop-off in regularity of your lovemaking. You may have to do a little coaxing, but as long as you're gentle and aren't probing you can get some sort of dialog going.

Once you've got him talking, listen. There may be more to the drop-off in your lovemaking than just not feeling in the mood. If someone is generally unhappy, they aren't going to be too enthused about sex. If you recognize a deep-seated theme, bring it up. He might not have even recognized it as the cause of your problems.

There can be a number of reasons why someone has lost that loving feeling. The sex itself might have lost its sparkle. As a relationship matures, so does passion. It doesn't mean the passion is gone. It just means you're moving toward the next phase of your relationship. Sex may just need some shaking up before that layer of dust chokes the both of you.

But not all bedroom problems have their origins in the bedroom. When we feel good, we want sex because it makes us feel even better. When we feel bad, sex seems like too much hard work. No one ever comes home from a miserable day and thinks, "I feel like getting it on."

Scheduling problems could be at the heart of your problems. I know it sounds lame (and it is) but jobs and life get in the way and suck up so much energy that the idea of fooling around sounds less appealing than a good night's sleep or a beer in front of the television.

A medical issue could also be to blame. If the problems lie with the guy, he's going to keep it to himself and let the issue eat away at him. It's what guys do. The problem can be totally nonsexual. Money worries and legal problems are real passion killers. When a person is preoccupied with a problem weighing on them, it becomes the only thing they can think about. It's a virus that can't be shaken off without help.

There's dozens of reasons why you two might've lost the lust, from the way you pick your teeth when you're thinking to the way he scratches when you ask him a question. Just spend time recognizing the issues. Don't pretend to know what the problem is and start offering your solutions. Depending on the issue, it could be like putting an electrical fire out with water. It's only going to cause more sparks. What you need to do is talk to each other, and listen.

"No, Really, It's *You*"

Be prepared for the truth to come out about how he feels about you. If you open up this line of communication, know that you could hear some things that you don't want to hear. Everyone hates criticism—especially when it's personal—and if it's sex related it's going to be super personal, with a side order of hurt feelings. Don't be tempted into a battle of wills where you have to one-up each other. This isn't supposed to be a blame game. Take any negative remarks on the chin or wherever they're aimed and deal with it. Just know that you can be just as honest and tell him a few things that may have him reaching for his protective cup.

Create a Balance Sheet

Take stock of your needs and his. Compatibility isn't a guarantee in a relationship; it's something you have to work at. What is it that you want from a caring relationship and where does sex and physical contact fit in? After talking with a few of my lady friends, there is an expectation that the frequency of their lovemaking will drop once the relationship stabilizes. Is this how you feel? Is this how he feels? There may be some disparity between the two of you on this issue. But don't interpret. The only way you're going to know this is by monitoring your sex life and talking to him. Before you talk it out, decide what you want and what you're willing to do to reach a compromise. You shouldn't be the only one willing to accept compromise. Look to him to make changes as well. You have needs too.

Seek Outside Help

You can always take your problems out of the bedroom and into a counselor's office, but I would urge caution. More than likely, he's going to resist taking this matter to an outsider.

The issue of not wanting to seek professional help is compounded by the subject matter. This isn't like you're asking him to do something about his anger management issues or drinking problem, where he's likely to see the sense of outside help. We're talking about sex. His bravado is going to shrivel quicker than his manhood after a quick dip in the Arctic. I can pretty much guarantee nine out of ten guys aren't going to want to discuss sexual issues with a counselor. Want proof? Here it is: If he's having trouble talking to *you* about the issue, he isn't going to want to talk to a stranger.

Again it's all about ego and pride. If he feels like he's failing in the bedroom, he's failing as a man, especially if his plumbing isn't working. There may be a trendy term in the form of E.D. and lots of supportive advertisements, but it isn't going to help much. Even if his equipment is working fine, this is a subject he doesn't want to admit to himself, let alone to you or any outsiders.

Yes, let's curse male pride and ego, but it doesn't change facts. He isn't going to like your suggestion to pop over to the shrink. If you can resolve this between the two of you, do so. It'll mean more. You're trying to fix something personal, not the air-conditioning or a busted transmission.

Put a Plan into Action

Once you're aware of your problems, you need to do something about fixing them. Put a plan of action together, but please, no pie charts and diagrams.

If sex has gone bad because of a lack of imagination then indulge in a few fantasies. Look back to the section on fantasies in the Sex chapter for a few ideas. It may be time to get your freak on and scare the neighbors.

If the reason for the sexual slump is to do with busy schedules, take time out for each other. Go on dates. And I mean *dates*. Have him pick you up from work and take you somewhere nice and then go home and show each other how much you care. Take weekend trips. Get away to someplace you want to visit for some alone time. It's hard to get distracted by life and monotony when they're a few hundred miles away. During these dates, dump your cell phones. This is about you and him—screw everyone else.

If you're looking at a medical issue, then it's about being supportive of each other. If it's him, show that you want to help get it resolved. If that means some hand holding and going to the doctor with him, so be it. He'll need reassurance. Let him lead though. Advise and counsel all you like, but let the decision to go see a doctor be his. He may want you to accompany him some of the way, but if there's a point when he wants to handle things himself, step back.

The same applies to you. If you have a medical issue, tell him. Keep him informed. Sharing this information with only your girlfriends, sisters, or mother does him a disservice. Yes, it's personal and yes, it's scary, but excluding him says you either don't value his opinion or don't think he'll understand. He can be many things and many of them dumb, but he can be your friend through challenging times if you let him. Let him help. Let him show his tender side.

Reassess

Re-evaluate the situation periodically. Just because you're breaking out the edible undies and the flavored lube doesn't automatically mean that everything is okay. Without cobbling together a spreadsheet, measure how things have changed. Has the passion returned? Is regularity up and nights in front of the television down? How has this changed from week to week? Don't presume initial results are sustainable. Just because you did it three times last week doesn't mean that everything is copasetic. It could be all back downhill again the next week. Also look to nonbedroom related results. Are the two of you happier? When people feel good, they show it, and when people are showing it in the bedroom, they're showing it outside of the bedroom.

Reassessing means keeping up the lines of communication. Keep talking and listening. You're looking for improvement. Where there is some, keep working it. Even when things do seem to be good, don't stop talking and experimenting. Keep running this little self-diagnostic program on your relationship. There's always going to be ups and downs in life and relationships, so don't put your due diligence on the shelf until the next problem arises. Stay focused on the two of you.

---

wrap it up

You and your guy deserve some fun in the sack (or anywhere else you desire!). If you're looking to take things to another level or rejuvenate your love life, there's plenty of ways to get both your motors revving. Don't let problems in the bedroom signal the end of you and him. You two can choose to do something about it. You just have to want it badly enough and when it comes to sex, don't we always?

CHAPTER 10

remain indispensable

You've become an important part of his life. You're his lover, best friend, and confidant. You've become all the things he seeks in a woman. You've reached a fabled position in romantic folklore—you're The One. All hail you.

Great. Fantastic. You've done it. You're The One. But there's one problem. You're his yin and he's your yang, but the longer he feels he's operating as a whole, the less he appreciates what you're doing. You've just wandered into dangerous territory, worse than a minefield or a shoe sale when you don't have your purse. You've made a serious error. You've become indispensable, but he doesn't realize it.

Now don't panic. This is a serious situation but not a relationship ending one—if handled correctly. The problem is you've created a comfortable environment for him. You've become a multifaceted person. You shift to suit his mood. When he needs a cheerleader, bang! You morph into one, mini-skirt and all. When he needs his fantasies indulged, bang! You slip into the

Princess Leia bikini. Wow, you're a great gal, but does he recognize that fact?

Now, he isn't necessarily being selfish here. He's more than likely just bad at subtext or a little dense. He knows he's got a good thing, but he doesn't realize he can blow it if he's not careful. As I've said before, women are the world's best communicators, but you can clam up at the worst times. When the stakes are high, you don't go to your men and lay it on the line for fear of failure. I understand. To you, you're having a heart-to-heart conversation. To him, it feels like an unstoppable asteroid on a collision course with the planet that will destroy him, all of mankind, and his DVD collection. Getting him to appreciate what he has without seeming like you're complaining is extremely difficult. So you may have to be a little wily when it comes to letting him know everything you do for him.

Treat Him Mean to Keep Him Keen

If he's taking you for granted, shake things up. Let him discover that there is no such thing as a self-emptying dishwasher. Now, throwing down your tools and going on strike won't help matters. You'll be seen as the aggressor and you'll be building a wall you can't climb. What you need to do is hammer home what life without you is going to be like, without letting your home go to shambles.

When people couple up, they tend to take on the relationship equivalent of conjoined twins. One half can't move without the other half coming along for the ride. The two of you have learned how to move as one. You're comfortable with this movement. There are tasks that one side handles better than the other. He leans on you for support without even realizing it. I say jerk the support away.

There's a number of ways of doing this . . .

Go on Vacation Without Him

Now don't use this as an excuse to go on that dream vacation spot the two of you have always promised to visit but can't necessarily afford. Take a trip that he won't necessarily want to accompany you on, such as a visit to out-of-state family, or attending a hobby-based convention he'll have no interest in.

Vacations like these are likely to keep you out of town for up to a week, which is plenty long enough for him to realize he's no longer his own man, he's part of a couple. He'll have to rediscover the skills he possessed as a male living alone. However, be aware of a couple of side effects.

Consequences to Fleeing the Coop
What's good for the goose is good for the gander. If it's okay for you to leave town for a long weekend, the same applies to him. Super Bowl only comes once a year and Tampa is a great place to be in February.

He's more than likely to struggle without you around. Don't expect to come back to a clean home. Expect a week's worth of mess. He's likely to regress. Food will be consumed from cans. Crockery and cutlery may have been tongue-cleaned for reuse. Deodorant is man's primary washing machine. The location of the trashcan will be forgotten. His new personal chef might be the fast food section of the Yellow Pages. Some command of the English language will be lost. While you may have to call in FEMA or alert a hazmat team, lessons

137

will be learned. He does need you. You are a necessary part of his life.

Stay Elusive

After a while, it's easy for him to get used to knowing where you are at all times. Your routine is just that—a routine. Monday at 10, you can be found here. Tuesday at 3, you're over there. You're as predictable as canned laughter on a sitcom. Because of that, you're the go-to kid when he needs something. You know you are. You're reliable and faithful. This means he can depend on you, but that's hard for him to do when you are as elusive as a politician's answer to a simple question.

While it's nice that you're around when he needs you, you can be taken advantage of. Your dependable nature makes you the person who will take up the slack. The worst part is that neither of you are aware that you're doing it. So don't let it happen.

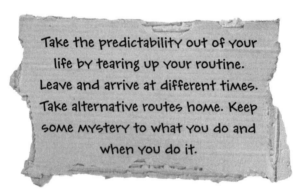

Take the predictability out of your life by tearing up your routine. Leave and arrive at different times. Take alternative routes home. Keep some mystery to what you do and when you do it.

Now, I'm not saying you should go out of your way to be elusive, but I'm saying you should be unpredictable. Unlike going on vacations without him, these are short, sharp reminders that sometimes he'll have to fend for himself.

Hit the town with your girlfriends. Keep it irregular. Never go out with them on the same night. One week it's a Friday. Another it's a Tuesday. Some weeks it's not at all. And other weeks, it could be twice a week.

Maintain your hobbies and interests. Do you like Pilates? Keep at it. Look for different classes at different times to prevent Tuesdays from becoming Pilates night.

Be spontaneous. Coldplay is playing tonight and someone offers you a ticket because someone else has dropped out. You love Coldplay. He doesn't. Don't turn it down because that's not what you do on Wednesday. If it's not conflicting with any other plans, go. He'll survive. He'll understand.

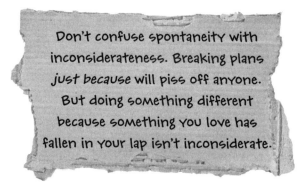

Don't confuse spontaneity with inconsiderateness. Breaking plans just because will piss off anyone. But doing something different because something you love has fallen in your lap isn't inconsiderate.

None of the above are supposed to send the message that you can't ever be relied upon. It's a reminder for him that you have interests that separate you for a while and that he'll be called upon to take on some of the tasks you usually handle from time to time.

Role Swap

Now, I'm not saying you have to go so far as to trade places with a stranger like they do on *Wife Swap* for him to appreciate your value, but I do say swap roles to break his dependency. We all fall into niches and patterns of behavior.

simon's story

Time for a Reinvention

Many years ago, I worked for a great woman called Liz. Liz was a sales manager at an engineering firm. She was sharp, capable, and inspiring. We got to know each other over the months then one day over lunch, she admitted she'd reinvented herself five years ago. Her reinvention wasn't her decision. Her husband had died. He left her provided for, but without a role in life. She'd played the part of the wife. She made the meals. She washed and ironed his clothes. She was mother to their children. For his part, he was the financial provider and rock. He went out to work. He controlled the finances. He balanced the checkbook. Effectively, he was her ATM. An old-fashioned relationship, yes, but one that worked for them.

Now without him, she was lopsided. She couldn't move forward, only turn in circles. She'd never had to worry about money. She never wrote the checks. She had no concept of bills and expenses. It took her awhile to adapt, but not long to flourish. She took on her deceased husband's roles, developed new ones and went into the workforce. I never knew Liz pre–her husband's death, but she assured me she was a very different person. Liz taught me that anyone can be anybody.

Now Liz's story may seem an extreme and a sad one, but hopefully you can see the parallels with your relationship here.

Couples complement each other. They are two pieces that form a seamless puzzle, but at the same time, those individuals need to know how they connect. Liz and her husband didn't learn that until it was too late. Love may be blind, but dependency can't be. You need to make sure he recognizes how lost he would be without you.

If you're the one who does the laundry and he's the one to brush the leaves out of the gutters—swap for a while. Let him realize the value of what you do and by the same token, you'll gain some understanding of what he does for you. Now, the swap doesn't have to be permanent. It might only take one time at cleaning the goop out of the u-bend in the bathroom sink to appreciate what an asset you are in his life.

Role reversal highlights the enormity of the contributions you make to each others' lives. When he sees the contribution you make to his life, it becomes hard to take you for granted and more importantly, you become someone he doesn't want to lose.

Just Say No

Like I mentioned earlier, couplehood can be viewed as becoming virtual conjoined twins. Where one goes the other is sure to follow. Because of this, there is a tendency for the +1 syndrome to develop. If he does it, you have to do it too. Over time, choice is forgotten.

For example, say his firm is sponsoring a baseball game. Spouses are welcome, but instead of asking you if you want to go, your name goes down on the list and why not, you're his +1. While it might be nice to go to the event, it doesn't interest you.

If the event doesn't appeal to you, say no. Let him go stag. He might not think he's going to miss having you there, but believe me, he will. Eventually he'll be done catching up with the people he knows and then he'll be left to eat alone while everyone else dines with their dates. And if you really want him to notice your value, let him go stag to an event where he's the outsider. He's going to miss not having you at his side.

Pigheadedness doesn't make the heart grow fonder, so saying no all the time isn't going to endear you to him. Say no when you really don't want to go and tell him why.

Learn to trade. This is really important. For some events he's going to want you to be with him. These events might be a snoozefest for you, but a schmoozefest for him. So recognize when it's important to him, but at the same time be ready to barter. If he wants you at the southwest regional dinner for bottle cap refurbishers, he can come to the local mall's spring fashion show.

The important thing here isn't to escape being his +1, but to avoid being thought of as an automatic couple, joined at the hip.

Don't Let Yourself Go

One thing *not* to do is let yourself go. This may come over as extremely sexist and shallow, but it's not meant to be. This is a very important. So I'm going to say it. You need to look good.

Now don't equate looking good with boob jobs, tummy tucks, and endless dieting. It doesn't mean you're doing your best to stave off time or compete with Angelina Jolie for who's the prettiest of them all. Looking good has everything to do with self respect.

Think about the dates you've had during your life. You dressed to impress. You bought something suitably slinky to cover that nearly there underwear and slipped on some high heels that hurt your feet, but damn they elongated your legs and tightened your calves to give them definition. You made sure your makeup was perfect and your hair was styled. Damn, you put a lot of effort into yourself and that was just for a date or hitting the town.

But something changed along the way. A date turns into a relationship. You get to know each other. You get comfortable in yourself. The effort you used to put in gets less and less. The high heels really hurt and the slippers with Mickey and Minnie on them are so much more comfortable to wear. It seems to be more effort than it's worth just to go out to dinner with him. There was a time when you wore that silk kimono-style dressing gown. Now you shuffle out to the mailbox in a terrycloth robe and flip-flops.

This sends a dangerous message to him. You've stopped putting the effort in. It says you don't care.

If you recognize this in yourself and you're not scared, you should be. This is a big step toward relationship termination. I'm not sure women realize what a slap in the face this attitude is to a man. You're an important part of his life. He wants to show the world he is successful. He defines himself by his job, his home, his vehicle, his possessions and by you, his lady. Now, I'm not saying he's trying to objectify you. He just wants to be proud of you. He wants the guys to think, damn, that Jim is a lucky guy. I wish I walked a mile in his shoes. He wants the women to think, damn, Jim's girlfriend is lucky to be with him. I wish I was in her position.

So when you don't look good, it reflects badly on him. Suddenly, he's not the guy often guys want to be and he's not the guy women want to be with. Questions start getting asked. "She's let herself go. I wonder if there's a problem at home?"

Women complain that men don't take notice of them, but that they'll look at other women. They're not going to notice you if you don't take any pride in yourself.

This initiates a vicious circle. You take less interest in yourself. He starts to take less interest in you. And it doesn't just stop with not caring about you. Anything you can do, he can do better. He'll stop caring about himself too. And so develops an uncaring battle of wills to see who can look their worst for each other. I think the winner is the first person to go an entire weekend without showering, or changing their underwear.

The Upside to Codependency

This is one of those rare instances where codependency exists in a relationship. If you give a rat's ass, he will too. If you care about your appearance and he doesn't, it shows. People look at you with a cocked eyebrow. She looks great, but did you get a look at him? This isn't like sitcom world where the tubby TV husband is teamed up with the dynamite wife. In the real world, someone would steal her away from him. Guys know this. When men feel they're losing their women, they'll do something about it. If you're looking mighty fine, he'll regain his six-pack abs that he let develop into a kegger. The way you look will determine how he treats you and himself.

wrap it up

All these activities are designed to remind him what life without you is all about and what it is you bring to the relationship. You want to be indispensable. You want to be his One. The problem is that once you attain that level, it's easy to take each other for granted. Sometimes, your partner will need a reminder. Absence not only makes the heart grow fonder, it also reminds him of how indispensable you are. If he doesn't want to lose you, he'd better not let you get away.

PART IV

how to stay with him

Girl has spent time with boy.

Girl wants to be in it for the long haul with boy.

Girl needs to think if she *still* likes boy—or leave boy.

CHAPTER 11

stop annoying him, he'll stop annoying you

Contrary to popular belief, men can do things without a woman correcting them all the time. I can hear you scoffing from here. Just stop it. Look at what man has done without any interference. Man invented the automobile (without which there would be no stretch limos). Man put astronauts on the moon (a great getaway to play some golf). Man invented the bra (and aren't you pleased about that). Man piloted the Titanic through iceberg riddled waters. Man built Pompeii next to a volcano. Ah, crap. Okay, a little female interference may be a good thing from time to time. But moderation, ladies. Moderation.

The longer people know each another, the more comfortable they become around each other. A side effect of this is honesty. People get so comfortable, they can tell each other anything. It's normal and healthy. It's inevitable that a woman is going to get comfortable around her man and she's going to start telling him where he's going wrong. This ranges from (but isn't limited to) how he dresses, how he does and doesn't fix things around the house, how he needs to get a better job or a promotion. This may all sound like useful advice to you, but to him this translates to, "You're a failure, can't you do anything right? Why am I with you?"

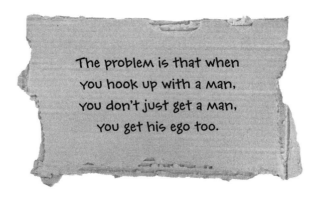

The problem is that when you hook up with a man, you don't just get a man, you get his ego too.

A Man and His Ego

Every time you offer helpful advice, it's a blast to his ego. Each direct hit hurts and he's going to either lash out at you, bottle it, or take it out on an inanimate object.

I know what you're going to say. "Men and their egos. Can't they give them a day off?"

The easy answer to this is no. Ego is an integral part of a guy. It isn't a pair of shoes that can be kicked off and left by the door after a long day at work. Male ego is like DNA. It's in every part of him from his little toe to his brain.

And who do we have to blame for this? No, not men, but our good friend biology. Biology dictates our core behavior, overriding intellect, and that's where ego hangs out.

I'm going to get all Discovery Channel here. Watch any animal courtship dance. It doesn't matter if it's birds, primates, or fish, it's the dude who's doing the dancing. His lady of interest is just watching the show, waiting to be impressed. A dude thinks he's hooked you because he proved himself better than all the other guys on show. Now he may not have danced to catch your attention, but he did something impressive which may have been something as simple as combing his hair that week. You know what you like about him that made you say yes to him.

So when a guy scores, his ego shines a little brighter, which probably accounts for the strut-like walk of a guy who's on top of his game. His confidence in himself and the confidence he radiates to the world is ego based. So when you interfere, your remarks are no different than shoving chunks of kryptonite in Superman's underpants. He thought he was the best on the block and you fell for him because of it, but here you are finding fault with him or what he does. Thanks for pouring a little salt on that open wound that is his ego.

Hopefully from this, you can see that interfering really can harm a relationship. Dependent on his tolerance and his confidence in himself, interfering can help turn that man of your dreams into the man walking out the door. Now, I'm guessing that you don't mean to interfere. You probably don't even know when you're doing it. Maybe I can be of assistance. Interference presents itself in a number of ways.

Stop Being a Nag

If he tells you to stop nagging, you've crossed a line. Nagging isn't a misdemeanor to a guy. It's a felony. It's assault with a deadly weapon. Every time he feels you nag, it feels like blunt force trauma. Someone call an ambulance! It's an emergency.

But in all seriousness, nagging is killer on a guy. When you tell him to go for a nice piece of salmon instead of the prime rib or tell him to buckle up, I know you're demonstrating you care. But listen to yourself. It sounds like he's a child and you're telling him to sit up straight and speak only when spoken to. It can come off a little condescending. He's a grown man. He knows what he's doing—sort of. If kept at a reasonable level, this is the kind of nagging he can live with. Where you ladies cross the line of helpful advice to full-blown nagging is when you interfere with something he enjoys.

If his passion is that Chevy Nova sitting in the garage under a silk tarp and he loves to spend his weekends under its hood gently caressing its caressable bits, telling him to stop spending so much damn time with that car (especially when you make the car sound like a whore), is going to set him off like a bottle rocket. It's not the fact you're asking him to spend more time with you. It's the fact you've put down something that makes him happy. It doesn't matter what it is. If it's something he holds in high esteem, it's going to piss him off.

Rephrasing can help here. If you want to modify his behavior, state what you want, don't go after his hobbies and interests. If your complaint is that he spends too much time with the guys, don't tell him you're tired of him hanging out with his deadbeat friends. You're forcing him to make a choice between his buddies and you. Instead, the reason you're complaining is because you feel neglected, so tell him that. Let him make the choice about what he sacrifices to be with you. He may very well cut the time down with his buds, but it's his decision and that's the crux here. Nagging is you telling him what to do. He's a guy. He doesn't get told what to do. He decides what he does. So work with his ego. Let him and it make the decisions. Your diplomacy can go a long way here.

Despite the felonious connotations connected to nagging, there is some good to be derived from it. Remember: a married man lives longer than his single or divorced counterparts. There are some beliefs in the academic world that nagging is partially responsible. The National Institute for Healthcare Research reported that divorced men are more likely to suffer from depression, die in a car, commit suicide, and indulge in substance abuse than married men. The reason for this is marriage and relationships come with responsibilities and obligations, which suppresses risk taking. And you thought he was irresponsible! Essentially, nagging reminds him that he has more than just himself to worry about and he needs to be careful. Nagging isn't just unwarranted complaining, it's a support system a single person doesn't possess.

Complaining that he looks like a slob on Sunday when he's watching football in the den is pointless (and obnoxious). Save your nagging for the important stuff.

So while nagging is an ugly trait, it does have its value and this is what you need to embrace. When nagging becomes nothing more than a series of demands or requests like, "Eat more vegetables" and "Have you seen a doctor about that third degree burn?" he's going to do these things begrudgingly. But, if you can sell him on the benefits of eating more vegetables and the drawbacks of gangrene, he's likely to obey. Nine times out of ten, what you're saying isn't wrong. It's the delivery that could do with a little help.

An Angel on His Shoulder

Another slice of interference occurs with you being in the wrong place at the wrong time.

Every guy loves it when his lady shows an interest in what he's doing. It's good for his ego and self esteem. This is doubly so when he's doing something tricky like installing a new furnace, changing a flat or successfully operating the washing machine. He's demonstrating his prowess with a difficult task and succeeding. You're impressed and he knows he's man among men. Remember what I said about this being like the Discovery Channel.

However, where this piece of relationship chewing gum loses its flavor is when this tricky task exceeds his skill set. Your hanging around him isn't such a good thing. The whole thing has become a pressure situation. Suddenly, your presence has turned changing a flat into diffusing a bomb. One mistake and it's a fate worse than death. He'll look bad not only to himself, but to you too. This is a massive ego dent. His place as your chosen male is in jeopardy. This may come over as unnecessary insecurity, but it doesn't mean it doesn't exist.

Where this pressure situation gets a shove into the stratosphere is when you offer your insights or worse, criticisms.

He can see the whole house of cards is teetering on the brink and he doesn't need you or anyone else to tell him this. This may sound harsh. I know you're trying to help, but you're not. You're just exacerbating the situation. You're bringing an open flame to a gas leak. There's going to be an explosion and you're in its path. Again, the problem here is ego. You're finding fault with him. He's losing his hero factor. The next thing he could lose is you to a more impressive male. In his eyes, quite possibly, this could be the repair guy who is coming to clean up his mess. This is survival, plain and simple, ladies.

Is this an exaggeration? Not as much as you think.

You know what it's like when the boss or a client is sitting on your shoulder watching everything you do, waiting for you to drop the ball and tossing in ill-placed suggestions. It sucks. It's uncomfortable, stressful, and frustrating. This is what it's like for him when you're the angel on his shoulder.

If you know he's operating outside his skill set, there are two ways of handling it. The first is to simply leave him to his own devices. Just occasionally check in with him to make sure he doesn't require any emergency surgery. The alternative is to acknowledge the difficulty of the task and tell him that you understand this is going to be a struggle for him and offer him your total support. It shows you care and understand the task is no cakewalk. It might also be nice to offer your assistance. A relationship is a partnership and showing you're willing to slog it out in the trenches with him is comforting and will help relieve some of his stress. This will be more appreciated than lobbing in advice grenades from above. It's more than likely he will decline your help, but the offer will go a long way. It's the thought that counts and all that. It might be nice if you offer him an out.

"Babe, you've never deactivated a nuclear bomb, have you? Shall I call the National Guard?"

Remember, one of your assets is playing the cheerleader. This is the time to embrace it.

Mistress of the Blatantly Obvious

It's an extension of the angel of his shoulder syndrome. Mistresses of the Blatantly Obvious go the extra mile. When all has gone wrong, these Pandoras of disaster feel the need to ram the dagger between the ribs.

This was my mom's super skill. The house could be a scorch mark in the dirt with burning insulation fluttering down like snowflakes. My sister and I could be standing at the side of the road, our faces covered in soot, looking like *Looney Tunes* characters. My dad would emerge from the wreckage and my mom's remark would be, "Cutting the gas line with the gas still running wasn't the right thing to do."

> Your man needs to know you still love and respect him despite his mistake. In fact, you need to show that you love and respect him even more for trying. If you can't do this, then stay quiet.

Hindsight is twenty-twenty but announcing it immediately after the mistake is cruel and unusual punishment. As

I've mentioned in the sections above, ego is at work. A mistake damages his ego. Having his lady pointing out his error to everyone is where ego-cide takes place. He knows he's made a mistake. He's lost face to you. He doesn't need it pointed out in glorious Technicolor, especially when you couldn't have done any better. How is hindsight knowledge helping anyone? Keep it to yourself.

My only advice here is don't be a Mistress of the Blatantly Obvious.

The Muse

If you are the interfering type or guilty of interfering, I do have one cure. It means a big change in behavior but it will put you in good stead. It doesn't matter how you dress it up, it's a destructive behavior. You need to turn your interfering ways on their head. The best way of doing this is by becoming a Muse. Muses were created to inspire the world to create masterpieces and invite genius. Behind every great man there is this great woman. That can be you. It doesn't matter if your man is Mozart, Da Vinci or Archie Bunker, you should be his inspiration to be better than himself. He doesn't have to go on to create great works of music that will transcend time, push thought beyond conventional norms or sharpen his bigotry skills. Just remembering to take the trash out the night before trash pickup will do. But let inspiration drive him, with you as its source, instead of tapping him on the shoulder every ten minutes to remind him of what he should be doing.

Whatever your man's heart's desire is (besides you, that is) inspire him to succeed. Take an active interest in his endeavor.

Quiz him on his progress, push him to make the next the step and wherever he needs an extra pair of hands, provide yours. Celebrate his successes and bolster him during the setbacks. You're still interfering with his life, but instead of prodding at it with a sharp instrument, you're getting involved, becoming part of the solution and not the problem. You'll be a good person to have around. To quote the great sage and personal fitness guru, Tony Little, "You can do it," and with you inspiring him, so can he.

Realize the Things You Do That Annoy Him

I've been married long enough to know there are two sides to every argument. And depending on the argument, some sides are weaker than others. I hate to burst anyone's bubble, but you aren't right all the time. On occasion, you set yourselves up for a fall. Now I know we had some fun picking on the boys, but some of your actions lead to his annoying behavior.

Let's have a look at when good girls go bad.

No Win Encounters

You tee up these explosive subjects for men and there is no chance of his survival. You don't see it, but he does. You've packed your deadly question into a shotgun, pointed it in his face and asked him to pull the trigger. He knows there's no way out. His pupils dilate. Sweat beads on his forehead. He tries to think of a nonincendiary answer, but it just isn't there. He's going to lose and he knows it. He's going to pay for this answer and keep on paying. He wishes he could keep his mouth shut but you expect an answer.

The two questions I'm thinking of are:

QUESTION 1:
"DOES THIS MAKE ME LOOK FAT?"

Wrong answer: "Yes."
Even if it is true or the honest thing to say, it's still the wrong answer.

Even worse answer: "No."
You know in your heart of hearts that he's being kind. You don't want kindness or flattery. You want honesty, while he wants an escape route.

QUESTION 2:
"I THINK SHE'S PRETTY. DO YOU THINK SHE'S PRETTY?"

Wrong answer: "She's okay, but she doesn't compare to you."
You know he's lying. If you think she's hot, then more likely than not, he thinks she's super hot and his imagination has just kicked in, so you berate him for it or sulk.

Even worse answer: "Yes."
That remark has just struck your insecurity gene and it's eating away at you. He's with you, but he's checking out chicks left and right. He doesn't like you. He doesn't love you. He's going to leave you at the first opportunity. So you berate him for his answer and sulk.

Please stop setting up guys like this. It doesn't help either of you. It scares the crap out of him and makes you insecure.

You wonder why men don't engage in conversation. The two questions above are a couple of reasons why. When any answer is wrong, the only safe bet is no answer at all.

Thinking He's a Mind Reader

I think you severely overestimate the power of the male mind. Let the words mind and reader be your guide here. Men have minds but they're quite happy not to use them. They wouldn't want to damage them. And guys aren't too into reading, unless it's the sports page or a manual and not always then. Who needs an instruction manual to hook up the DVD player anyway? It's really intuitive, isn't it?

I've witnessed the expectation of male mind reading powers quite a bit. I consider myself pretty sharp and quick on the uptake, but even I get lost. A girlfriend or wife will impart some vital information but it'll be wrapped in a thick layer of subterfuge. This subtext isn't malicious. It just is. This hidden meaning is completely lost on the male. He takes what he's told at face value and accepts it, only to find he's totally missed the point. He's an illustration from my friend, Jemise.

simon's story

We Do as We're Told

I used to live with this guy and we were planning a party. We had just moved into our apartment during a snowy winter in Philadelphia. My girlfriend was over to the house and per normal, we all divided responsibilities so that we could get everything accomplished. Because it had been snowing, I suggested that we buy "something to cover the floor." I assigned this task to my roommate and then dedicated myself to my chores for the party.

After a day of shopping with my friend, we finally arrived home. We only had about ninety minutes before the party and we were quite pleased at how well things had gone. When we opened the door, we found that the carpet was covered in ripped brown paper bags from the grocers. I found him at the table eating as if he had done a great job with preparing for the party.

My initial reaction was, what the hell is this? And his response was, "You told me to cover the floor so that people would not track snow in and ruin the carpet." "Yes, but I meant for you to buy a rug." Then he says, "But that is not what you said." For me, it was tacit that one would buy a rug when expecting company and not cover the entire party space with brown paper bags.

Any woman who heard me say, "pick up something for the floor," would have understood that meant a rug. My girlfriend did. But my roommate didn't. It goes to show that women infer one's intentions through conversation while men can only follow specific instructions.

Jemise nails it here. Men will do exactly as you say as long as you say it. If you turn something as simple as taking out the trash into *Moby Dick*, it'll be done wrong. Plain speaking works every time.

Not Saying What You Mean

Men are busy. They have TV to watch, trash to forget to take out and experiences they need to exaggerate. As a courtesy, they would prefer it if you say what you mean. When you don't, it isn't a lot of fun for him. He feels like he's been suddenly transported to Bizarro World where everything means the opposite of what it really does.

Men may still possess Neanderthal tendencies, but they do a pretty good job of picking up on mood changes. So if he asks you, "Are you okay?" and you say, "I'm fine," he's going to leave it at that. Guys have no problem bottling emotions and keeping things to themselves. If he doesn't want to talk about something then it's not coming out, not even under torture. It just isn't done. And when he picks up on your mood shift but you say you're "fine," he thinks you're doing the same. He's not being uncaring or insensitive to your feelings. He's just giving you room to work it out on your own, because that's what he would do if he were feeling the same way. Coming after him two hours later to chew him out over his insensitivity may make sense to you, but it won't make sense to him. You said you were fine. If you weren't, you should have spoken up, and he would have gotten involved. He would have listened (or at least attempted attentiveness). All you had to say was, "No, I'm not fine. I'm mad as hell and I'm not going to take it anymore." Men understand straightforward. They can work with that. And when they understand what you want, they will be able to better address your concerns.

Men get accused of not expressing their feelings all the time. This isn't a lot different. Essentially, when you don't say what you mean, you're masking your true intent in ambiguity. Let's face it. No one likes ambiguity—by definition it's tough to get a handle on it. Make it easy on everyone and say what you mean.

Overanalyzing What He Says

There's a tendency for women to overanalyze what men are saying. You obsess and twist yourself into knots unnecessarily. You're looking for hidden depths to something a guy says. But words like hidden and depths don't go together when it comes to men. Face value is your friend here.

When a man tells you something, he means what he says. If you ask him does he prefer breast or thigh for his chicken dinner and he says thigh, then that's just exactly what he means. He's not making an underhanded remark about your legs. He just likes dark meat. And don't go reading anything into that statement, either.

If you want to know what he thinks about your legs, ask him, "What do you think of my legs?" I know this could be viewed as one of those "no win encounters" that we discussed in Chapter 1, so remember not to load the question.

---

wrap it up

Well, that's you, ladies. You're not as perfect as you think you are, but that's okay. Nobody's perfect. We all have faults. Knowing that means we can give each other a little slack, and we can move forward. Let's go.

As I was writing this book, I noticed an interesting thing about these pet peeves. The complaints about men are directed at the action or inaction of men. Why do men do this or why is it men can never do that? The complaints directed at women, however, are based on what they do and don't say. Why do women say this or why is it women can never say that? Men embrace action and women embrace words. This could be a key to greater understanding.

CHAPTER 12

don't be the jealous type

At the beginning of the book, I listed a bunch of pet peeves women have about men. One of the pet peeves I didn't mention—because I felt it deserved a chapter all of its own—is *your jealousy*. And now that you've found Mr. Right and decided that he's The One, you better work on not letting that jealous side shine through and ruin what you have got going.

You have to realize: Guys are going to look at other girls. I'm guilty as charged. There's no getting away from it—we're going to look. We'll sneak a peek at a hot girl walking down the street even if we have to do it through sunglasses or catch her reflection in a store window. She doesn't even have to be three-dimensional. A guy will sit forward in his seat when his favorite female movie star comes on screen. (Salma Hayek is my personal Achilles heel.) And his fantasizing doesn't stop with the movies. There are plenty of girls that grace the pages of *Playboy* and *Penthouse* that have him thinking not so pure thoughts. So when it comes to looking at other women, men aren't short on opportunities.

The problem is that men are attracted to women. If we see one we are particularly attracted to, we are going to look and appraise—*especially* appraise. However, it's not just about looks. I'm not sure women realize this. A woman doesn't just catch a man's eye because of her physical appearance. Men aren't *that* shallow; they're just a *little* shallow. Men are drawn to look at a woman because of the way she moves, the confidence she exudes, the way she dresses, and the attention she commands, all adding up to her overall sexiness. As we've discussed, it's a lot more than just looks that makes a woman sexy.

Time for a Little Context

So you catch him looking at another girl, what's the big deal? Are you telling me that you don't have fantasies? It's only natural. The key difference between men and women, however, is style. Men are open books. They're easy to read. When he's checking out a girl, you know it. Women are far subtler. If you see a guy in the street and you think he's attractive, your man isn't going to notice you checking him out. This is because you aren't going to go slack-jawed at the sight of him. You're sly about it.

> Don't be naive and believe that just because you're a couple, he'll forget other women exist. You will still think about other guys being attractive. It's important to realize that looking is perfectly fine.

So let's all be honest and admit that he's going to check out ladies and you're going to check out guys. Just because you've partnered up with someone in your life doesn't mean you're going to put on a pair of blinders and pretend the opposite sex doesn't exist anymore. It's just not realistic.

Say you see a hot guy with a striking resemblance to Brad Pitt walking down the street. You get a tingle. Now what? Are you going to act on this desire? Are you going to blow off your relationship with your man because of it? No, of course you're not. Nor will he when the same happens to him. Don't equate his looking with cheating. We don't live in a society where you are guilty just by thinking of something.

Let him look.

Give Him Your Blessing

The problem with getting bent out of shape when he looks at a pretty woman is that it gums up the lines of communication between the two of you. That's no good. Men already get a bad rap about internalizing their feelings. So if you blow up every time you catch him peeking, it isn't going to get him to open up at all.

And if you think he isn't going to look just because you say so, think again. You're dealing with the laws of nature, so there's no point in blowing this out of proportion and turning it into a huge fight. You're not going to win. Let's face it: Prohibition doesn't work. They tried with alcohol and what happened? It forced boozing to go underground. The same is going to happen with him. You're going to force him to sneak surreptitious looks and enjoy these moments behind your back. This only helps build a wall of silence and encourages deception, which isn't going to forge a long-lasting relationship.

Be Open about It

Keep your knee-jerk reaction to yourself and learn from this situation. Ask him why he's into this woman. You might find some key insights into your man when it comes to women and what attracts him, what his fantasies are, and what he finds sexy.

Of course, you'll scare the crap out of him if you suddenly ask him, "Why are you looking at her? Do you think she's pretty?" This comes off as accusatory and will frighten him into not responding honestly. I suggest that if you catch him looking at another woman, you look too. Then say, "I think she's very attractive." You've given him the green light to look. He'll be comfortable with that. He'll tell you what he thinks. Do this a couple of times and he'll see that you aren't threatened by his looking. Instead of snapping on a pair of sunglasses to sneak a peek, he'll let you know when he's looking at a woman.

Remember to volunteer your own insights. I've learned a lot from my wife about other women. I'll point out a woman that I find attractive and she'll remark about the sun damage on the lady in question. She's also got a great eye for surgical enhancement. My wife can spot fake boobs at 300 yards. We are now very open about who catches our fancy, and it keeps any sort of secrecy removed from our relationship.

You know better than he does how well a woman ages, the tricks of the trade on looking good, and hiding flaws. Not only is this a nice demo of your inside knowledge, but you shape how he views women. Guys are easily blinded by the glitz and glamour of a woman's looks. An insightful remark helps him see beyond a hot pair of legs or a great rack. You let him see how a woman changes and how beauty changes. It will be quite an eye-opener for him.

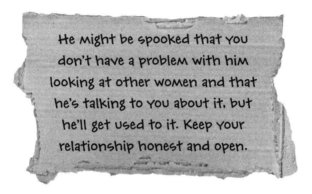

He might be spooked that you don't have a problem with him looking at other women and that he's talking to you about it, but he'll get used to it. Keep your relationship honest and open.

Insecurity from Your Jealousy

Acting insecure is a *big* turn off. Like complaining, it's draining because it means more work for him. Your man can't be himself around you if you fly off the handle when you spot him checking out a girl or he talks about a new female friend. In the back of his mind, he'll be continually wondering if you'll be pissed off if he says this or that. Effort that could be put into pleasing you is now spent avoiding potential conflicts.

Let me be brutally honest here: There's a big difference between him checking out a girl walking by and cheating. And what have you got to be insecure about? He's with you and he wants to be with you. (If you find his plans for a tunnel escape system though, you *might* have something to worry about.) Come on, you know you're stronger than this.

Keep It in Check

You are a strong and secure woman. You let your man look; you even discuss the ladies he's checking out—but don't let it go too far. Moderation and respect is everything. You can't allow him to get out of hand, so be prepared to set limits. There is a big difference between checking out a girl and ogling. Ogling tends to involve noises, possibly grunting, and drooling. It is also disrespectful to you and the other woman.

Some good guidelines to institute are:

- *No* yelling out at her or making noises as she passes
- *No* making gestures of any kind
- *No* walking ahead of you to make her think he's single
- *No* exchanging numbers or handing out business cards
- *No* investing in a telescope or night-vision gear

Remember, it's fine for him to have urges (and you as well). The problem is if he acts on them. Telling him he can't have these types of urges might be the thing that pushes him to act on them. However, allowing him a restricted space to have them will help your relationship.

> You can't expect him to bottle up his lusts and expect the bottle not to burst. Letting him look is fine. It's not going to drive him away. It's going to drive him to you. You're cool. He's going to love that.

Don't Let Jealousy Ruin
Your Relationship

Jealousy has to be the most volatile element in the relationship universe. Once the green-eyed monster has emerged from the swamp of mistrust, then there's no coaxing it back to its home. Jealousy, regardless of whether it's justified or not, is a mortal wound no relationship can survive.

I hate jealousy because it's so destructive. I've seen a number of my friends' healthy relationships hit the rocks over it. Either they've been the victim of a partner's jealousy or they've been the jealous one. I've even been the victim of jealousy. I hate it when I see Salma Hayek out with other men or when she ignores all my phone calls and e-mails. (Call me, Salma. *I miss us.*)

While jealousy has its place, it's usually over nothing. That's the annoying thing about jealousy—it's based on perception. You perceive that something's wrong: He spends too much time with his friends, which means he enjoys himself more when I'm not with him; therefore, he's cheating on me. This last one is the biggest killer of relationships. Hear me now: Perception is *not* truth. Do not confuse it with such. Perception is a feeling at most, an un-founded belief at worst.

As women, you pride yourselves on your communication skills. You talk. You listen. But when jealousy has women in its grips, your best skill takes a vacation. You stop talking and start internalizing. This ignites your imagination and you create conspiracies and scenarios. People become chess pieces you move around a fictitious board in a game just to prove you were right. Effectively, you've turned yourself into a guy. You've bottled up all your fears, you're not talking to him, and you're letting the situation poison you.

I have only one piece of advice: *Stop it!* No good can come from feeling this way. Let's look at the components of jealousy. Hopefully, if you understand them, you can avoid them.

Mistrust

Trust, like respect, is earned, but everyone deserves the benefit of the doubt. You have to go into the relationship with a certain amount of trust. If you don't think this guy is honest and decent, why are you in a relationship with this person at all? If you don't have trust, you'll never be happy. You'll be a nervous wreck because of it and—no matter how you slice it—it's going to be a miserable experience.

simon's story

Suspicions—the Relationship Killer

Insecurity usually features at the heart of a lot of jealous feelings. A good friend of mine ended up in what ultimately became a doomed relationship. His girlfriend never trusted him. She didn't like it when he talked to other women, professionally or casually. She'd check up on him and obsess in social situations. Her fear was he'd cheat if she took her eyes off of him, even for a second. At the heart of this wasn't a track record of him running around on his girlfriends, but an ex-girlfriend.

My friend had ended a fairly long-term relationship with his high school sweetheart. Life took them in different directions and they broke up, but they remained in touch, Christmas cards and birthday phone calls—that sort of thing. Every now and then they bumped into each other on the street, but they never met socially beyond that. However, my friend's new girlfriend couldn't accept the relationship for what it was. She tied herself into knots imagining how he'd cheat on her. She went to the extent of checking itemized phone bills and quizzing his friends to see if he'd actually been with them when he said he had. It was an uncomfortable relationship that lasted several years before it came to an end.

Did my friend's girlfriend have good reason for her suspicions? No, and I'm not saying that to take sides. As the outside observer, I never saw my friend ever exhibit any signs that he wanted to run back to his high school sweetheart. It was over in both their minds. She represented a pleasant memory of good times had. It can be argued that my friend's only crime here was that he still associated with his ex-girlfriend. However, this isn't something I prescribe to.

His Past History

Everyone has a history. Unless you were there at someone's birth, that someone will have loved and associated with someone before you. You aren't going to be someone's first and only love. If you can't accept this then things are going to be rough.

Ex-partners are tricky ground. There is the possibility you're the rebound girl. However, as the current girl in your man's life, you aren't the one with the cause for concern. He's with you. You're the alpha female. He dumped her and chose to be with you. It may seem extreme to think like this, but think about it. He's with you. Accept it. Live with it. Embrace it. If he really wants someone else and they're available, why stick with you? There's nothing to hold him. You don't have anything to be insecure about, but if you continue to be insecure, you will drive him away.

Your Past History

Insecurity may have a foundation if you have a past history of bad relationships. If you've been cheated on in the past, you're in a fool me once, shame on you frame of mind. You have your antennas tuned to cheaters. That's fine. That's understandable. But to instantly label every man who comes into your life as a cheater will only cripple the relationship. You have to let the past be the past and go on faith that your new guy is being honest until he proves how trustworthy he really is. There's nothing worse for a guy who hooks a great girl only to have the scars of her past relationships ruin any chance of a successful one with him.

Taking "Advice" from Others

Ask ten people to give you an answer on a subjective subject and you'll get ten different responses. Everyone is an individual and they all see the world differently. As a wise man once said, "Opinions are like assholes, everyone has one and they usually stink." So true. So true.

While going to others for answers can be helpful, it can also be confusing. So if you feel your jealous side coming out, seek help. Sound people out, but choose wisely when it comes to sharing your problem. Look at Othello. He listened to Iago, a trusted friend, but Iago was bitter—bent out of shape by his own jealousy—and look how that ended up for ol' Othello. So vet who you take your advice from. If you seek help from someone who is jealous by nature then there's a good chance you're going to get a slanted answer. That said, it's good to seek advice from someone who's got a few relationship battle scars. However, you need to be sure the person you're seeking advice from is someone you trust. Their insight is just as valuable.

Misinformation

Don't let misinformation drive you crazy with jealousy. If someone tells you that your guy has a reputation for being a real lady-killer, consider the information and compare it to what you know. Maybe your friend's sister says she saw this guy over the weekend who looked like your guy kissing some girl. Even if you feel there's something to a claim, don't take it to be the truth. If you weren't there, you don't know for sure. Give him the benefit of the doubt until proven otherwise. There's nothing worse than being accused of a crime you didn't commit—so don't fall into the trap of believing in hearsay and rushing to persecution.

If you have a concern, investigate. You don't have to launch into a congressional hearing or anything, but bring the issue to his attention. If he's fibbing to you, you'll be able to tell. Guys don't make good liars. Generally, innocent people get angry when they're accused of something they didn't do. Guilty people get defensive. Liars concoct cover stories, but rarely think them through. "Where were you?" "At the movies." "What did you see?" "Um…" A liar's body language is very different to an honest person. They struggle to make eye contact. They place obstacles between you and them—such as tables, a room, or continents. Before launching into a full-out assault, investigate, talk to your guy, and trust your instincts.

Fulfilling the Prophecy

He's going to cheat on you. You're convinced of it. It's happened before and it's a matter of time before it happens again. You're so convinced of it, you're forever telling him this. You might even take it a step further by following him or even setting him up to test his fidelity.

If you've been cheated on, I can understand how this can be a fear. It sucks when it happens. It's a betrayal and a sledgehammer blow to your self-esteem. It's a fear worth mentioning to him. "Hey, babe, I got cheated on before and I don't want it to happen again." But this is a remark you mention once. You don't go into the relationship with the expectation that you will get cheated on.

If you keep harping on this thought of possible infidelity, it will create a miserable situation for him. He knows you're obsessing about whether he's cheating on you. It's going to wear on him after a while. It doesn't matter what he does or what assurances he gives, he's guilty, so why not do what he's being accused of doing? This is a weak response on his part, but I've known it to happen. A jealous girlfriend hammers her guy about his fidelity when he's been loyal and eventually, he surrenders and does cheat. Both parties are at fault here as both have torpedoed their relationship.

If you fear being cheated on, get a grip on your fear. Don't let it wreck what you have going. Judge your guy on his merits and not on your neurosis.

> Yes, your guy can cheat on you. It's regrettable and sad—and I hope it never happens to you—but if it does, you have to do what's best for you. Move on and look for better because you deserve better.

Be Up Front

If something he does is eating away at you, talk to him. Jealousy seems to have the effect of sealing lips. You clam up and look for signs of his betrayal. The only time you do say things is to jab away with a snide remark. This serves only to piss him off. If you have a genuine concern, confront him. Say in plain English what it is that is worrying you. If you don't like that he hangs out with his old girlfriend without you around, say it. If you don't like that he's always painting the town red with his buds on your dime, then say it. It'll make for an uncomfortable conversation, but it's no more painful than ripping a Band-Aid off real quick. It'll hurt for a second but it'll be over. That's a lot better than letting bad thoughts and feelings fester for months. Remember, guys don't always pick up on your subtleties. A passive aggressive remark dropped here and there will only confuse him. He may not even realize that he's doing something that is causing you pain.

You need to have honesty in your relationship, not jealousy. If you feel yourself getting envious, do something about it. It's the only way your relationship will work.

---

wrap it up

Jealousy is a nasty cocktail—one part self-doubt and one part mistrust. It's a hard drink to swallow as it doesn't look good and tastes even worse. Save yourself and the one you love from its intoxicating effects. No one needs the hangover.

CHAPTER 13

become his dominant female

Your relationship has matured. You two are comfortable around each other. You've got a good routine working for you. You know each other's ins and outs. It's nice. You like it and he doesn't complain. But, I have a few questions for you:

- ❏ Do you dress him in the morning?
- ❏ Do you wipe his chin when he spills his food?
- ❏ Do you send him off to work with a pat on the head and packed lunch under his arm?
- ❏ Has your sex life dwindled to something that can be called occasional at best?

If you've answered yes to two or more of these questions, congratulations! You've just become his surrogate mother. Hmm, doesn't it feel good? Probably not. I'm guessing you didn't sign on for mothering duties this early in the game.

Let's not start pointing fingers at who's to blame. It takes two to tango and all that. Women are nurturers by nature and men like to be nurtured. Okay, let's have a look at the situation here.

The Male Component

Men are raised by women. Now, I know it's the twenty-first century and we can pretend that perfect equality and division of labor exists, but there's no avoiding the jobs and skills Mother Nature gave us. Women are the ones who carry children and give birth. They're the ones who produce milk. Equality is never going to change this. Nor is the nurturing nature of women going to change. Women are still more likely to be the stay-at-home parent, make the meals, and administer medicines. A mother's love is a mother's love. As much as a guy might try to emulate this, he will always fall a little short. A dad's love is different—as it should be.

With the case for political correctness left licking its wounds, let's get back to men and their needs. There's something very comforting about a woman taking care of his soulful needs. And yes, these are soul-based needs. It's good for the soul to have someone kiss the boo-boos better and make a meal for you. This need for comfort will rise with the stress level in your man's life. Careers seem more stressful than ever. The higher a guy rises through the ranks, the tougher it's going to get. Decisions need to be made and those decisions affect people and money. Success comes with gray hairs. Look at any U.S. president. They look like their own father by the time they're rotated out of the system. Even if a guy isn't rising up the ranks, there's still stress. Jobs these days seem to be as easy to hold on to as a greasy pole.

So you can see how a little bit of a mother's TLC would do a guy a whole bunch of good. There are an interesting number of high-flying businessmen who get their rocks off playing the submissive to a dominatrix. Sometimes guys want someone else to take control of the reins . . . and the handcuffs.

This is where you come in. No, not as the dominatrix, although that's always an option! It's easy to see why your guy put you in the mother position. In some ways, you've taken over from his mother. The serious girlfriend or wife becomes the primary woman in his life. You've taken the throne from the queen. As such, you're the one he turns to, to catch him when he's falling. Take it as a compliment. When he grazes his knee, it's your name he calls and not mommy's.

This is my personal point of view, but I prefer to be looked after by a woman than by a dude in times of strife. When I've been confined to the hospital, I've wanted a female nurse to attend to me. Now that isn't just because I have a penchant for sexy uniforms. It's just a fact. I don't mistrust male nurses or anything. It's just that I'm scared because something is wrong with me and I'm instantly put at ease by a female presence. When a lady nurse tells me it's all going to be okay, I believe her. If a guy nurse says this, I don't quite believe it. I think it has to do with my belief that a female caretaker wouldn't lie and if they did, it'd be for my own good.

Also, let's compare bedside manners. If a kid takes a header in the playground, scuffs his knees and grazes his hands, what's the mother's stock reply? "Let mommy kiss it better." That's a beautiful thing. That's love. What would a dad's advice be? "Walk it off." That's just what someone needs to hear at that moment. Walk it off, for God's sakes. Walk what off? That doesn't sound like medical advice to me. Do you see the difference now?

The Female Component

Women are nurturers. It says so in your DNA. You care for yourself and for those important to you. Guys tend not to be this way. They don't even look out for themselves. Statistics bear this out. Single guys don't fare as well as those in relationships. Guys in relationships have someone looking out for them.

Take this incident between my wife and me a few years ago. We were out walking the dog around a lake and my wife scooped up something and cradled it in her hands like it was a broken heart she'd found in the dirt. She proffered it up to me like Oliver Twist asking for some more.

"Bird's nest," she says, like that explains everything.

"I see that," I say and shrug my shoulders. I'm a man of the world. I've seen bird's nests before.

"Where are the eggs, Simon? Where are the babies?"

Now, I'm a caring person. Really, I am. I've fostered dozens of animals for the local pound, but I saw the bird's nest and I didn't see what my wife saw. She saw a family in possible distress. I saw an old bird's nest. No casualties were involved, or if they were, it was too late for them. Effectively, my mind had decided to tell the birds to walk it off. When did I become such a meanie?

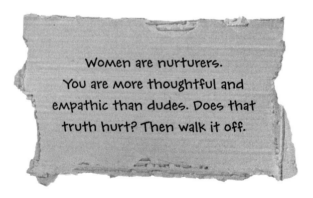

Women are nurturers.
You are more thoughtful and
empathic than dudes. Does that
truth hurt? Then walk it off.

Empathy plays a role here, in that women possess it in spades and guys have a small consignment. A guy's empathy is centered on real problems and issues. Guys are empathetic when it comes to a bad golf game and when his best bud is going through a divorce. If a guy gets downsized, his buds are there. Where a guy's empathy dries up is when situations get a little wispy around the edges. If a guy complains he feels he's losing his way in the world and it's time to change direction or his identity is in crisis, his friends are likely to tell him to, "Walk it off." It isn't that guys are unsympathetic. They're just very grounded and practical people. A guy is better off taking a "what if" issue to a trusted female. She's going to offer advice and solace to soothe his soul in a nonjudgmental environment where whatever is said isn't going to be mocked.

A woman's caring nature shoulders some of a guy's burdens. Guys exhibit their own "Walk it off" mentality. If they need to take medication on a daily basis, there's usually a woman shoving the pills into their hands. Women know it's important to look after one's self. Guys want to plow on and hope the issue takes care of itself. When a woman intervenes on a guy's behalf, he's happy with the result. The pressure of the problem has been removed and now someone else is caring for the problem, allowing him to keep moving forward. Consider it emotional outsourcing. If you have a strong nurturing gene, it works for you and it works for him.

For guys, women are a safe place for shelter. You are not only compassionate, but you take an active role in curing what ails them.

Understand His Mom, Understand Him

A boy and his mom—it's a pretty tight relationship. Just look at Norman Bates and his mother. Men might not want to admit it, but women play a strong role in their lives, and the first lady of their world is their mom. It doesn't matter if she was a great mom, a mediocre one, or even a damn right terrible one; a guy gauges other women by his mother. So don't underestimate her importance.

A mom is double-trouble for you, the significant girlfriend. She's raised him and instilled him with preconceptions of what is going to be. She's the gold standard by which all women are measured. If that wasn't a tall enough order, she continues to have an influence over him even as an adult. If you don't come up to scratch, her disapproval could have a detrimental effect on your relationship.

Without getting all creepy and Freudian, a guy's mom is his first love. She fulfilled all his needs. She nurtured and protected him from harm, oriented his moral compass, and gave love unconditionally. Sounds like a tough act to follow—and it is. Because if you're going to become his *One*, you need to equal anything his mom did. Anything less and he'll be left unsatisfied.

If you're going to be the woman who becomes his serious love interest, you're going to be the one who breaks that first love. So, it's important how you handle his mother now that you're looking to take on part of her role. You need to watch, listen, and learn because when it comes to sons and mothers, there are lines you don't want to cross and lines that can never be uncrossed.

Look to His Mom

To see where you fall on the mother standard, you need to see her in action. Now, I know how this sounds. Everyone is skittish about meeting their significant other's parents. It feels like you're on trial. You can feel them judging you on everything you do from the way you dress to the way you eat your soup. Even if it's well meant, there will be an inquest after you leave. Who needs that kind of scrutiny? It's understandable that you may want to avoid these encounters, but don't. If you do, you can't get a gauge for his relationship with his mom and—more importantly— you can't get a close up look at the way his mom operates.

This is where you need to go into Discovery Channel mode—listen and observe. Watch how she interacts with your man, and how he interacts with her. Look at how she makes him happy and how she makes him sad. Recognize the differences between how you and she treat him. What you see in her will tell you a lot about how he likes to be treated. For instance, you might notice that he likes to be babied, but doesn't like too much physical affection. You can use that to your advantage. Whatever you find out is worth noting.

Now, the point of this isn't to become a carbon copy of his mom with the one key difference being you can have sex with him and she can't. The point of this anthropological exercise is to understand where you stand. You've got a few options here.

Option #1: *You can emulate her, which may seem the safest option.* But if you become too much like her then it's going to creep him out and you'll lose him. Another problem with this approach is that you're stifling your own personality, and do you really want to do that?

Option #2: *Draw the line in the sand.* It's you or her. However, while being your own woman is commendable, it doesn't necessarily help you either. You're asking him to choose sides. Now, that's fine if he doesn't like his mother, but it could also be a relationship-ending move on your part. Remember, he's known his mom longer than you. She has tenure. All you have is that funky little thing you do with your tongue that he likes. In this cage match, it's unlikely you'll win.

Option #3 (the *smart* option): *Take the best parts of his relationship with his mom and incorporate them into your relationship with him.* If you notice that he hates it when his mom criticizes the little things, don't fall into the same trap. If you see that he likes it when she praises him for his little successes, why not do this? He'll love you for it. This way, you'll develop a relationship with him that rivals his mom's and may even top it (probably on account of that tongue thing).

Stay on Good Terms with His Mom

I'm an advocate of staying on good terms with his mom. I don't mean suck up to her and pretend to be her best pal. I mean be friendly and open with her. Remember birthdays and anniversaries. This will help you in the long run. You'll be accepted faster and if you're accepted, he'll accept you even quicker. You've been given the *Mom Seal of Approval.* What boy isn't going to listen to his mom on that score?

If you build a friendship with his mom, you gain a valuable ally. Is he not fulfilling your needs? Not listening to you? Not looking after himself? Call in his mom. This is where her tenure works for you. She'll help lay down the law and get him compliant. That's what moms are for.

Bad Mommy, Bad

But what if you and his mom don't get along? Maybe you've tried the olive leaf thing and it hasn't worked. Fine. You did your due diligence. Just keep your dealings business-like. She is someone you have to do family business with, so stay civil.

She may be trying to push you out, so she can stay his #1 girl. Don't be drawn into an argument. This will reflect badly on you. His mom isn't stupid. If she doesn't like you and she wants to show you up, she'll set you up for the big fall. She'll bait the argument with enough poisoned meat for you to bite. "You're not as cute as his previous girl. I always told him he should have married Jane. She was such a nice girl." If you snap at this bait, you're the bad gal. The best result in an argument like this is that both of you come off looking bad. It's a pretty hollow victory.

Don't trash talk his mom on the car ride home. It doesn't matter if you're right. You're taking a swing at his mom and he's going to defend her. This can be very tempting when she's trash-talked you, and your man—her boy—didn't come to your defense. Remember two things. First, you're a big girl. Suck it up. It's a petty outburst. You'll live. Defend yourself where needed, but don't argue. Second, state the facts—not emotions.

Say, for example, she called you out for not having a job, forcing her boy to care for you financially.

Don't hit him with, "Why don't you ever stick up for me? Why do you always take her side?" He's going to hit back with, "My mom was right, you do complain too much."

Do tell him you didn't appreciate the remark or the fact that he didn't tell his mom you're studying for a degree like he was a few years ago when you were supporting him.

He isn't going to want to pick sides, so don't make him.

The same applies even if he can't stand his mom. Let him trash-talk her, but don't join in. It's not your fight. Butt out. I'm serious here. You're crossing a line where you have no chance of winning. Talk trash to your pets to bleed it out of your system. That's what they're for. I advise against talking it out with your girlfriends. This stuff has a habit of getting back to the source. Just be understanding and supportive. Show him that you're a better person than his mom and leave it at that.

And, no matter what you do, never trash-talk his mom when they're both present. You are the outsider in this relationship. It's them against you, especially if he's got siblings. You can be the nicest person in the world, but you're going to come off ugly and you'll lose. Don't be the one to turn Christmas Day into an episode of *Jerry Springer*. It'll be a pretty lonely place.

If you're dealing with a difficult mom, don't get suckered in. If you can keep your tongue while she's running her mouth, she'll be the one that will come off looking bad. Hopefully, he'll see his mother's shortcomings and if he's forced to choose sides, he'll choose you.

Don't Forget about Dear Ol' Dad

I've talked a lot about moms, but what about dads? They're people too. Don't you have to win them over as well?

Yes, you do, but in general, dads are much simpler creatures and easier to win over. Since dads are men, flattery goes a long way. He has an ego. As a guy gets older, his shine might fade, but his ego still needs feeding. He wants to show that he's the block that his son was chipped from. As he ages, a dad can feel like he's lost his importance, so recognizing that he exists and throwing a few kind words in his direction will go a long way.

Play to his interests. If he's into something like music, movies, or sports and these are things you know well, you've got a talking point.

Be nice to your guy's dad, but don't play up to him too much. Dads are crappy at hiding their feelings. If he's getting too much fun out of having you around, mom is going to notice and she might not be pleased. You might be winning over the dad while pissing off mom. This is the worst way to make an enemy of her. So, acknowledge his dad, but don't turn matters into a soap opera.

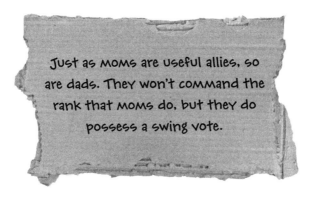

Just as moms are useful allies, so are dads. They won't command the rank that moms do, but they do possess a swing vote.

Rome Wasn't Built in a Day

Now all this may sound like you've got to come out of the gate running and your first day on the job as his new girlfriend is to get to his mom, impress her, and then be twice as good as her all before bedtime. While that would be handy, it isn't going to happen, nor is it expected. This is a relationship. It needs time to develop. He isn't going to dump you right away just because you didn't know how he likes to be burped after dinner. He isn't Donald Trump.

No, the situation is that somewhere along the line, you impressed him, so much so that you started dating. This begins your voyage of mutual discovery. You both are getting to know each other on a much deeper level. As this relationship becomes more complex, the two of you decide how important the relationship is going to be. During this build up you should be observing his mom and taking your cues from her. You need to build toward surpassing the gold standard of mom. But don't be in a rush to have this angle covered immediately. Women are complex people—including his mom. You're not going have a handle on her or have her won over quite so fast.

So that's his mom. You can't ignore the way she's treated and raised her boy, your man. She's had a powerful influence over him and has shaped how he sees women and how they're measured. She possesses the power to ruin your chances of a long-lasting relationship with him. However, she's not the enemy; she's actually a very important ally. Take into consideration how she treats him and you'll realize how you should treat him. Figure out the amount of nurturing he's used to and supply the same amount. Don't underestimate the power of his mom—unless you want to lose him.

Much Love

The upshot of your nurturing ways and his need to be nurtured can force a loving relationship to go down the wrong route. Essentially, it's a case where too much nurturing has created an identity crisis. You've lost your identity as a girlfriend who nurtures and become a nurturer who happens to be his girlfriend.

It's easy to see how this happens. You are going to be the dominant female in his life. There are no ifs, ands, or buts about it. You're his go to girl for affairs of the mind, body and soul. This means inheriting some of the nurturing role previously held by his mother, but you want to be in it as his soul mate, not his unpaid help.

Obviously, something has to be done about the situation.

Turning coldhearted to dial back on your nurturing ways isn't going to help. It's not going to snap him out of it. He'll still want someone to look out for him and if it's not you, he'll look for it elsewhere.

The key phrase here is "someone to look out for him." Guys like having someone looking out for their best interests. No one said that his #1 woman in his life has to do everything for him. That's the key difference between you as his girlfriend or wife and his mother. A loving mother will do anything for her offspring to ensure he gets the best start in life and is able to survive on his own two feet. You, on the other hand, aren't there to continue raising him. Yes, you've taken over from his mother, but only in a supervisory role. If you feel you've become too much like a mother and less like a girlfriend, examine what you're doing for him. From the moment he comes home, is everything in his life catered for? Here's some behavior to watch out for:

- ❑ Does he remember to take his medications or do you hand him the pills?
- ❑ Are you making all his meals?
- ❑ Are you buying all his clothes?
- ❑ Do you make his doctor and dental appointments?

If you're making these decisions or others like these about his well-being, then you're doing too much. Being a sympathetic and caring partner is one thing, but babying him is another. The remedy is simple: Stop treating him as your child. Be a supervisor. Tell him to take his medications, but don't do it for him. If he's going fishing the next day, you can remind him he needs to sort out food for the day, but don't load up a cooler with a feast. If he balks, remind him you're his girlfriend, not his mother. It's a cheap line, but it puts things in context.

Every guy wants a gal who cares and someone who'll listen to him in times of crisis, but don't become his nursemaid. He wants someone he can depend on, not someone he's dependant upon. His mom brought him up to stand on his own two feet. The more you treat him like a man, the more he'll remember you're his woman.

Become His Strong Female Presence

Powerful, forward-thinking women get a bad rap, mostly because it's hard to settle on a term for them that isn't *bitch*. One term that encompasses this female leader position is matriarch, but it has a somewhat stuffy sound to it. It's reminiscent of family dramas on *Masterpiece Theater* featuring a domineering woman who barks orders from a chair that looks like a throne. It's hardly the image for a modern lady such as yourself, but the role of matriarch is something you're likely to face, as you become the leading female force in his life. You now sit on a throne beside him as the matriarch of coupledom.

I'm not sure if we have things any harder than previous generations, but the world does seem to be more uncertain. Jobs for life no longer exist. Terror plots dominate the news. Foreclosures are at an all time high. And *Dancing with the Stars* will return for another season. This is scary stuff. A guy has to navigate his way through these shifting circumstances. This is where the matriarch comes in.

A guy needs a strong presence with him to ride the storms life throws at him. He doesn't need a matriarch to fight his battles for him, but what he does need is to know there is someone looking after the home base while he's trying to get ahead. This doesn't mean he wants you barefoot and pregnant at home. The mortgage is too high for that. It's a double income world. No, the home base isn't just a physical place, but a state of mind too. Home is wherever you two are and his job isn't. Home is a safe haven. And that safe haven requires someone to look over it. That's the role of the matriarch and that's your role.

Now you may be asking yourself if you really want this job, but try to recognize this road sign in your relationship's journey. Men will want you to take on a certain matriarchal role in their lives. Don't get scared. He's decided you're strong and good enough to be the dominant female in his life. He's putting his faith in you. You're on your way to becoming his one.

The matriarch is a position that comes with a job description. These are some of the tasks to look out for.

The Mother

A guy never really severs his maternal ties. He just reattaches them to another strong female figure. He needs someone with soft edges when times are rough. He's looking for someone to comfort him, take care of him when he's sick and who makes dinner when he's hungry. Now, none of this is necessarily because he's lazy. He's looking for the ability to be able switch off from the daily grind. You and your nurturing skills can provide this. It's nice to be able to leave his troubles at the door and shut them out. He's no longer beholden to anyone and can be himself. He can get a backrub, foot massage, or hug (not necessarily in this order or at the same time). This is man pampering. Whereas you might get a pedicure, manicure, or facial to indulge your needs for rest and relaxation, a guy just needs some TLC at home.

This may seem a little lame and a cop out, but there's more than a grain of truth to this. As we've gone over, stats say married men live longer than their single and divorced counterparts and are less prone to depression and alcoholism. I believe this has a lot to do with them having that mothering aspect in their lives. They have someone to go home to and seek solace from. Since dudes having pedicures isn't as yet socially acceptable, single men don't have a good outlet for their stresses. So, life either eats them up in the form of depression or they seek a little escapism at the bottom of a bottle. It does make you wonder if the rise of the metrosexual is an outlet that bridges the gap between a single guy needing a feminine element in his life. I'll let you ponder that one.

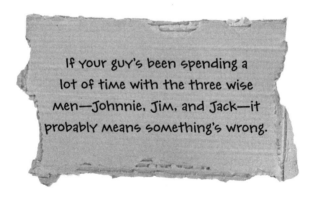

If your guy's been spending a lot of time with the three wise men—Johnnie, Jim, and Jack—it probably means something's wrong.

Also, I think the lack of an outlet is generally why men don't bounce back from divorce or the break up of a long-term relationship as well as women do. Men only have women for their outlet, whereas women have other outlets. You're self-starters like that, but boys need a little help. Can you help out?

Advisor

This is where you demonstrate your tougher side in the role of advisor. He is faced with decisions daily. Some are easy, such as: do I want the forty or eighty team package on my sports cable subscription? Answer: eighty. Some are hard, such as: can I get away with wearing this pair of boxer shorts for another day? Wrong answer: yes. Right answer: seek advice from your girlfriend. The problem with decisions is that it's hard to tell which is the right one until it's too late. He can sit for an hour chanting red wire, blue wire, red wire, blue wire, with the time ticking down, but it's so much nicer to be able to turn to someone for their opinion.

This is where you come in with your two cents worth. You're the matriarch, the tribal leader. Your view on any subject is valuable. The role as an advisor carries weight.

Again we're in a comfort zone. There's something comforting about being able to talk through a problem or an issue with someone he trusts. This isn't just because a problem shared is a problem halved. Your opinion is biased for the right reasons. You don't want him to make the wrong decision. Because of that, you're going to seek the best possible solution. If the decision is a workplace related issue, you're a go to person. Your advice isn't tainted with office politics. You'll see matters for what they are. Even if the decision to be made is personal or on a topic he knows well, he'll want to seek your counsel. Your insight is important.

The most important reason why he seeks your advice is because you care. You care about him and what happens to him, more so than anyone else. Your advice is going to be heartfelt and honest.

He'll also go to you for advice because some of his choices will affect you too. While it would be nice to make those decisions by himself, any unilateral decision could come back to hurt you as well as him. No longer do his actions impact only him.

Even if he doesn't take your advice, your role as an advisor isn't diminished. It's good to have a sounding board to bounce ideas off of. You've helped him come to a decision in a relaxed environment and that's the important thing.

The Authoritarian

This is where you get to practice some tough love. Men are notorious for not taking the advice of doctors or other authority figures. They don't take their medications or vitamins. They don't eat the right foods and they binge on the bad stuff. If there's a right way of doing something, they don't. Essentially, you're dealing with a kid with a driver's license. Sometimes he'll need a timeout to bring him into line. You're the one who has to make sure he takes care of himself.

Your authoritarian skills are also needed elsewhere. Guys procrastinate. If there's a job that needs doing and doing well, it can sorta, kinda wait for some other time. You need to crack the whip now and again—and if you can wear knee-length, spiked-heel boots while doing it, it'll go a long way toward making sure the task gets done.

Your authoritarian side goes a long way toward preventing guys from regressing. A woman's presence helps to keep him from reverting to his primitive instincts. A sink becomes a limbo world for dirty dishes. Direct hits to the toilet while peeing are preferred, but aren't necessarily mandatory. Underwear can be worn until it makes a cracking sound. I, myself, as a bachelor used put off vacuuming until it sounded like I was walking on a gravel driveway when I crossed the living room. This doesn't happen now that I have my matriarch. It could also explain why we have hardwood floors and not carpet in the house. Either way, it's a win-win.

The sterner side of a matriarchal side is needed. You're his check and balance. He needs a regulator, someone who will tell him what to do—not necessarily do it for him.

---

wrap it up

At the beginning of this section, I talked about the importance of the mother figure in a guy's life. She's the gold standard by which all women are judged. His allegiance is to her. But by the time you've reached the matriarchal stage, there's been a shift. The torch has been passed from his mother to you, his partner. His mother will always have a strong place in his heart, but you are now the dominant female in his life. He's made a choice. He's committed to you. Wow, it almost sounds like he's beginning to grow up.

CHAPTER 14

either work it out,
or break it off

As a relationship develops, you and your beau will see more of each other. The dynamic changes significantly when you go from dating to moving in with each other. The time spent with each other goes from two or three times a week to every day. You're together when you go to sleep and you're still there when you wake up. If it wasn't for jobs, you'd be in each other's company every minute of the day. So you can see how this can be a little claustrophobic.

Now, giving each other space doesn't just apply to when you and he have moved in together. This applies to the dating stages too. No doubt you've seen it yourself when couples have become inseparable and one of them doesn't seem able to take a leak without the other being there. It's sickening, isn't it?

The Rocky Side of Relationships

So you two like each other. You like hanging out with him all the time. What's the problem with that? Nothing at all, as long as he feels the same way. If he doesn't, get yourself a life vest, you're going to hit the rocks. And when that happens, you have to decide whether it's time to batten down the hatches, or abandon ship.

Following are a few of the typical situations that guys see as choppy waters. Learn from what other women have done wrong and find out how to help your relationship survive.

The Smothered Stage

Generally, guys like their chicken smothered, but not their relationships. This will scare a guy off faster than if you pulled out a couple of snapshots of your kids. Park rangers warn tourists not to corner a wild animal. The same applies to men. While you might think it's cute that you're always around, he might not. The problem is that smothering is highly subjective. What you think is reasonable might be totally different than what he thinks. Here are a few things that can get you into trouble:

The Me Syndrome

The flip side of smothering someone with too much love and affection is turning needy. You feel like you're giving your all and you're not getting enough back, so you go on the offensive. Your attitude becomes, "Screw him. What about me? Me! Me!! Me!!!"

He books a table at his favorite steak house for the two of you, but you insist on going to the French place he doesn't like. He wants to see a movie, but you want to go clubbing. He makes plans to visit his family at the weekend, but you force him to break these plans to be with you. The only friends he has are your friends. He can't have a dog because you don't like them. Sex is when you say it is. Whatever he wants doesn't matter, it's all about what you want. You give him no due consideration. You're the star.

Yes, he's with you all the time, but he isn't with you because he wants to be, but because he's tethered to you.

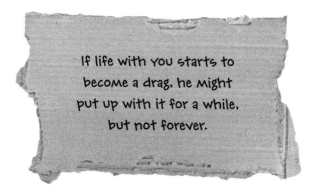

If life with you starts to become a drag, he might put up with it for a while, but not forever.

Going *Way* Too Fast

Whether you're dating or living together, watch your speed. You may be going too fast. How long was it before you started moving your stuff into his place for sleepovers? Who was the one who decided you should move into together? Who said you should see each other more often during the week? If you're the one who is controlling these decisions then you might be going too fast for him. Check his enthusiasm levels at all these stages. If he's just as excited as you, then keep your foot planted to the floor. If not, ease up off the gas there, Danica. For a whirl-wind romance to work, both of you need to be caught up in the moment, but if he's running off to the bomb shelter, you may want to back off. You don't have to back off completely, but you need to find a speed that you're both happy traveling at along the relationship highway. Eventually, he has to be comfortable when you maneuver him into the diamond lane.

Pushing Each Other's Buttons

Subjectivity. I'm going to keep mentioning it, because it needs mentioning—a lot. The Imelda Marcoses of you out there think 300 pairs of shoes aren't too many. Normal people, such as myself, think four pairs are more than sufficient. When there's only you to consider, subjectivity doesn't matter too much. You want to own 300 pairs of shoes? Go do it. But this type of decision matters when you're in a relationship. I don't care how matched the two of you are. Your perceptions of appropriate behavior are going to be different than his.

You think you should go out together six times a week. You call him several times a day. These things might sound reasonable to you, but he might not think that way. This could be way too much. He might be too nice to say anything to you, but there are ways of recognizing when you've crossed a line.

- ❑ Does he avoid your calls?
- ❑ Does he find excuses to break dates?
- ❑ Is he less affectionate with you publicly and privately?
- ❑ Is he annoyed when you spring surprise visits on him?

If you're answering yes to these questions, you're pushing his buttons in all the wrong places. Now this isn't to say he doesn't love you or doesn't care about you, but you're scaring him.

Look at your behavior. How has it changed? Compare your relationship now with two months ago. He could be avoiding your calls because you call twice as much as you used to. Talking to you should be a joy, not an inconvenience. You used to meet for lunch a couple of times a week, now it's every day. This could be taking the fun out of seeing you. Remember, you're not the only person in his life. He has friends and family. If you're encroaching onto the time traditionally spent with them, then he's going to resent your time together. And don't underestimate the power of friends and family. If they start pressuring your man to make a decision about who he spends his time with, then it's going to come back to hurt you. So watch your boundaries. Don't let yourself get carried away. What's your rush?

The Sacrifices You Have to Make

You've given up doing things you enjoy doing and spending time with your friends and family, so why can't he? Excuse me? What did you just say? You've given up hobbies and interests that made you happy? Why on earth did you do that? You're entitled to your pursuits too. Who said you had to give anything up for him? You're in a relationship. You haven't joined a convent.

Part of a relationship includes sacrifices, but only as part of compromise. You shouldn't surrender everything important to you so that you can be with him every second of the day.

Losing Your Identity

Neither of you should lose your identity. You're a couple. Great! But you're still two people. No one is expecting the pair of you to merge into one being or to stop being yourselves. If you feel you've become a different person since meeting your guy then it's time to re-establish who you are. He fell for you for the person he first met and that person no longer exists.

Don't ignore yourself just so that you can be with him 24-7.

So not giving him enough space is going to crush any burgeoning relationship you are developing. Okay, just saying you're going to give each other space is one thing, but it doesn't carry much weight. Giving each other space requires understanding and ground rules. Let's start with understanding. You're into your guy. He's the greatest thing to come along since the latest pair of Jimmy Choo's and you want to be with him more and more, but his damn family, friends, hobbies and job just seem to be getting in the way. Don't be selfish, he deserves a life outside of you. Consider these issues:

He had a life filled with people before he met you. You are not a substitute for them. You're an addition to the family. If you can't accept that, you should go looking for your next man at an orphanage.

He has hobbies. Hobbies make people happy. If he's a basketball or baseball freak, you know he's going to want to catch a game or watch it on the TV. You take that away and he's not going to be happy. Look, he deserves hobbies and interests. You don't have to pretend to understand them or like them, but understand that he does and let him have his fun.

You don't own him—unless you can provide me with a receipt of purchase. Your man is not a pet. He may have some nasty habits you associate with pets you've owned in the past, but you didn't buy him. He doesn't have to perform for you at your instruction. It would be nice, but it ain't going to happen.

He's his own man. Remember, you fell for this guy for who he is. You start stripping that away and you'll end up with someone you don't recognize.

If you keep crowding him, he'll be unlikely to show his true feelings because he won't want to upset you. This will be especially true in new relationships. Use your powers of observation to gauge his feelings. Look for tension and frustration when you demand more time or tell him he can't do something he's been looking forward to. Know when he genuinely wants you to tag along and when he doesn't. "Sure, it would be lovely if you came along to the strip club with me and the boys, my sweet."

Now, if you think any of these points are unreasonable, turn the tables. If he treated you this way, how would you be reacting right now?

It's one thing to be understanding, but you're going to need some ground rules. Yes, there were lots of things he used to do before you two kids hit it off, but now there are two of you and he's not just thinking for one, but for two. Two—this may be a tough concept for him to understand, but he'll get it with a little bit of help from you. If you don't establish ground rules, there's a good chance that you'll end up as a doormat. You'll be so understanding that he and everyone else in his life will walk all over you.

Okay, let's talk about ground rules. You're a secure and independent woman. You recognize he has things in his life that extend outside of your lives as a couple. You want him to be himself just as much as you want him to be the man at your side. Good. That can work if he knows the rules:

Rule #1: Don't let him weasel out of chores. Make sure that his excursions to see his mom, hang out with the boys and hit the lake for some fishing aren't being used to avoid hanging out with you or chores he doesn't like doing. Men can be wily, but these deceptions are easy to spot. His regular Thursday night poker game shouldn't change nights twenty minutes before the two of you were supposed to be going out that evening. And you should only fall for "Monday night football is being played Tuesday this week" once.

Rule #2: Every good turn deserves another. So, you indulge his passion for baseball or fishing. Baseball and fishing seasons are by nature seasonal. There is a whole big chunk of the year where his passions aren't in season. This is where you come in. You cut him slack when his passions are happening, but when they're not, he has to defer to you and your needs.

Rule #3: Set limits. If he's restoring a Chevy Nova, make sure it happens in the garage and that it doesn't break ranks to invade the kitchen, the bedroom and the backyard. If you're the couple with the cool plasma TV, don't let him turn the place into a frat house when his buddies come over for the game.

Some guys are real social animals with a ton of interests. It seems if they aren't indulging their passions for sports, clubbing, or hanging with their friends, they're out doing something else which either excludes you or makes you just one of the crowd. This leaves you wondering where did the "you and him" time go? Now, if he's an everywhere man, he's going to be keeping a calendar to stay abreast. Well, if all his fun time goes in the book, you go in the book too. You're important. Insist he list you among his appointments. Not listing you may not be intentional, but out of sight is out of mind, making it easy for him to forget you had plans. I'm not a big fan of couples scheduling their time together. Dear, can you make it Friday at five for a deep meaningful discussion? I think so, pumpkin, but only if we can meet at my office. *Brrr! Formality gone frigid.* However, this could be the wakeup call he needs. He'll think, "Wow, she needs to make an appointment to see me."

Give Him His Space

Don't let distance be confused with thinking he doesn't care. You have lives together and lives apart. Live them both. I don't like it when I hear either a man or woman complain they don't do the things that made them happy before they met their partner. That means something has gone wrong. Both of you need to do things outside of each other. It's healthy and normal. Don't confuse it with anything else.

My wife thinks I'm the bee's knees, but she doesn't want me in tow every minute of the day. She thinks I'm special, but not that special. She has plenty of things she does without me.

The nature of my job takes me on the road a lot, meaning I'm gone for days at a time. I have fun when I'm on the road. I get to meet new people and hang out in unfamiliar places. Even though I'm having fun, I'm thinking about my wife. I go home with a bunch of things to tell her. She could come with me on some of these trips, but doesn't. While it's fun for me, it's not fun for her, so she doesn't come and I don't force her. If the places I'm visiting appeal to her, she'll join me at the end of the trip and we'll do Simon and Julie things.

If you're a couple, you're a couple at all times, whether you're in the same room together or not. Nowhere does it say you have to be tethered together 24-7. A bond of love can be forged into a shackle of resentment if handled poorly. Even a shadow releases its hold when the sun goes down. Give him space. Give yourself space. There's a reason why they say absence makes the heart grow fonder.

When It's Time to End It

Relationships are difficult propositions. Divorce statistics prove they're prone to failure. No one likes failure, but relationships aren't like piloting an airplane or conducting brain surgery. One mistake isn't going to result in a fireball or someone eating through a straw for the rest of their days. Relationships can and will fail. They can even run their course, coming to a natural but satisfying end. You shouldn't be afraid of failure. It's not a bundle of laughs but it's not the end of the world. Okay, it might be embarrassing and painful to end a relationship, but is that worse than staying in a miserable place? Too many times women stick around for the wrong reasons, thinking they can't do any better, or believing they can change him, or some such excuse. As much as no one wants to admit it, sometimes it's better to walk away.

How Do You Know It's Broken?

Every relationship has glitches. You argue over something meaningless. He forgets your birthday. You didn't remember to TiVo the *Gilligan's Island* marathon. These are hardly things to pack up your stuff over. Issues that negatively affect your overall happiness, however, should have you pulling the suitcases out of the closet. This book has discussed a truckload of stuff that you can do to hook and win a guy, but it's only one side of the story. For everything you do, you should expect something back in return. You go out to the ball game with him and make his favorite dinner. He surprises you with tickets to see your favorite band or books a romantic getaway. Whatever it is, you're going out of your way to make him happy and he does the same for you. It isn't cool if you're going out of your way and he never bothers to do anything for you. A relationship isn't about keeping score, but it isn't about someone taking all the time either. If you're giving all the time and not getting anything back, then you've got a problem.

Neglect is a nasty turn in a relationship. This is where one of you totally ignores the other's needs. It goes beyond taking from a relationship and not giving. You may be two people living together, but only one believes the other matters. I have a friend whose relationship went into decline. They'd been living together for about a year, but they'd lost that loving feeling somewhere along the line. He'd go out with buddies without telling her and come home late. This cycle of forgetting that she existed continued. She decided to win his affections back with sex. He was lying on the sofa watching TV and she climbed on top of him. She began to undress him and make some moves. He responded by rolling her off the sofa and onto the floor so he could continue watching his TV show. If that isn't a sign, I don't know what is.

Abuse, whether it be physical or mental is never acceptable. People will argue, voices will be raised and things may be thrown in frustration. These are things that happen, but they're heat of the moment things. You get angry and you calm down, but if it goes beyond that, it's time to pack your bags. There's no excuse for violence or acts of humiliation. If someone abuses you or you abuse someone else, it's time to go.

How to End It

You know something is wrong between you and him, so do you just pull the trigger, kill this relationship dead and move on? No, take a moment. Look at what you used to have between the two of you and what you've got now. Make a list of where you two have gone off the rails. Seeing your problems in black and white helps you put things in perspective.

The next question to ask yourself is do you want to put things back on track? If you think with some tweaking, you can get your relationship running smooth, then it's worth doing, isn't it?

You've assessed how you feel, now for the tough stuff. Talk to him about the way you feel and the changes for the worse you've noticed. Even if he's neglecting you, there may be a relationship worth saving. Guys get wrapped up in their own lives and that makes them dense to everyone around them. They may not even know they're doing you harm. Also guys are not talkers. His turning away from you could be indicative of his fears. He may be worried things are moving too fast and this is his way of slowing things down or it could be something outside of your relationship that's sucking up his energy. Either way, get to the bottom of the problem. But if you've tried getting through to him and you've tried to make changes for the better and it's all failed, then jump ship.

Hopefully, he'll respond to you pointing out that you two are in trouble, but there's also a chance he's not interested and he doesn't care. Then, whether you like it or not, you have hit the end of the road. If it isn't working for you, then go.

Check your happiness barometer. If the needle is pointing to storm clouds all the time instead of the smiley sunshine face and you can't see a way of swinging it back, then you've got a problem. Happiness is a state of being we all should strive for; after all, life is short and can only be made longer by misery. That's not a great way to attain immortality. If your job sucks and it's bringing you down, then change jobs. If you don't like where you live, move. The same applies to relationships. If you're miserable and you can't see a way around it, break up.

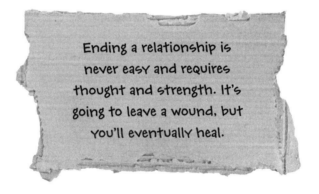

Ending a relationship is never easy and requires thought and strength. It's going to leave a wound, but you'll eventually heal.

Make a Clean Break

Okay, you've decided it's over. You want to start fresh and meet someone more compatible. This is the real tough bit. Actually ending it. It's not going to be fun, but you have to be courageous. You have to actually say the words, "It's over." There can't be any confusion. There's no good way, but some ways are better than others.

Be Direct

If you want to end the relationship, tell him face to face. No post-it notes on the refrigerator for him to find when he comes home to an empty house or letters from lawyers. The only exception to this rule is if you suspect he may become violent. But at least leave a phone message explaining yourself.

Don't be ambiguous. I can't stress this enough. Too many women don't want to hurt their man's feelings or try to soften the blow, so they wrap the discussion up in vagaries. They say things like, "Things aren't working out right now, but that doesn't mean I'll always feel that way." He walks away thinking he's still got a chance when there isn't one or wondering whether the relationship is really over. The more humane thing is just to say it straight. Don't disguise what you mean.

Where to Break the News?

Choose a place for the break up where both of you are comfortable and there are no distractions. This may be in your home, but your home can dilute the importance of what you're saying. Your home is a familiar place and the break up loses significance It can be seen as just another argument at home. So what's new? Instead, take him somewhere quiet you can talk. I would steer clear of restaurants because if it turns into an ugly scene, no one needs to see it. And don't take him to one of his favorite places to do it either, or broadcast it over the public address system during a Yankee's game. That's just cruel.

Tell Him What Went Wrong

I say this for two reasons. You guys didn't work, but hopefully he can learn from his mistakes and succeed with someone new. And again, it removes the element of ambiguity. You are leaving him because he never does anything for you, he doesn't pull his weight, he's inconsiderate of your feelings, he's unsupportive of your career, he demeans you in public, etc. Whatever the reasons, tell him what they are. This isn't so you can be vindictive, but as I've said before, guys aren't mind readers. He may not even be aware of his behavior. Now this isn't an excuse, but if he isn't aware, he should know. You might even ignite an epiphany. He might surprise you and want to change his ways.

Of course, if you catalog his shortcomings, be prepared to receive a list of yours. Don't get angry or defensive, just listen. There are may be some valid points in what he's telling you.

Be Adult about the Breakup

Don't tell him it's over by introducing him to your new man or having one of your friends or family members tell him. Breakups are bad enough. They don't need an element of revenge.

Also, keep it civil. I know that's easier said than done, but if you take a methodical and reasoned approach to breaking up with him, it's harder for a war of words to break out. It won't enable you to leave with smiles and hugs, but at least your CD collection won't be thrown out. At the end of the day, you may not leave as friends, but you should be able to bump into each other on the street and not unleash a bout of Tourettes.

---

wrap it up

Relationships fail, but that doesn't mean you're a failure. You shouldn't stay with someone if you're miserable. Happiness should be your life's goal and a good relationship factors into that equation.

boys will *always* be boys

Well, that's men for you, ladies. As a breed, we aren't perfect and never will be, regardless of how much the women in our lives try to change that. You just have to accept that men have flaws and there are some things they'll never get right. When you think of them in that way, I think you'll come to find that they're quite endearing.

There is no great secret to men. They're straightforward people with simple needs. They want to be cared for, but at the same time, made to feel they're their own person. They need to be secure that someone is there for them, without feeling like they're being pinned down. A little bit of juxtaposition, I know, but that's guys for you.

Men aren't just looking for a copilot who will help steer a relationship through the waters of life. They're looking for added value. They're looking for a woman who makes them better than they already are. Men know they're flawed. They know they're not great at looking after themselves or the best at maintaining a clean and livable environment. So they're looking for a woman who compensates for their shortcomings. The ideal relationship for a man is like a two-piece jigsaw. They're one half of the puzzle, irregular with gaps and tabs that stick out and they're looking for the other half of the piece who can match them perfectly, filling the gaps, providing recesses for the tabs and removing the irregularities.

Women seem to miss this key male need. Instead, you see his flaws and irregularities and think you can do something to correct these imperfections and change him into your vision of the perfect man. This is square peg in a round hole thinking. It doesn't matter how many times you smash Mr. Square Peg into the round hole of female philosophy, his head isn't going to make it through the hole. It'll just give him a concussion. That's why a lot of men walk around with a permanently perplexed look on their faces, especially the ones who've been married a long time. It's probably the reason why men tend to go through second childhoods. It's brain damage.

The problem with trying to change a guy is that you run into his wing man—ego. Guys are slaves to their egos. Guys don't drive around in pickups with monster-sized wheels and gun racks for nothing. Even seemingly egoless guys have them in some form. Ego helps men find their place in the world. It determines pecking order. There isn't anything wrong between two guys fighting for dominance to show who is number one. That's nature and it goes back to the caveman days. What doesn't work is you whomping all over his shortcomings with a stick like he's a piñata. He won't want to see his ego broken open and watch you devour the candy inside. Just acknowledge that a guy has certain sensibilities like you do. If you don't tell him he's good for nothing, he won't tell you your butt's too big. Deal?

And if things get a little bumpy on the way to long-term bliss, communicate with him. Sure, bounce ideas and thoughts off your girlfriends, but don't let them be your only source of information. They'll only see things from a female perspective. Make sure you have a couple of honest guys on tap who'll put you on the right track. But for the real dope on your guy, go to the source. Talk to him when you have a problem, and remember, these talks should be open communication—so no issuing of ultimatums, and you need to listen to what he's telling you as well as talk.

For a modern relationship to survive, it needs to look to the past. Equality today has been taken too literally. Dividing life down the middle doesn't always work in a relationship. A couple has to complement each other. You are strong where he is weak and vice versa. That's relationship equality. Equality comes from making each other better. That's love and that's what men want.

The reason guys are a little shaky on the commitment front is faith. They have to believe they've found the only woman who can fulfill him. A guy has to know that there's no other woman in the world giving him what you're giving him. You have to make him realize that you're *it*. He won't get anyone better. Convince him of that and you've got him.

Now that you know what to do, go get him!

index

about the author

SIMON OAKS was born and raised in England. He grew up in a world dominated by women in the form of his mum, sister, aunts and a host of female cousins—none of whom thought he was listening while they were talking amongst themselves. He's partial to Special-K—and looks great in jeans because of it. He now lives in Northern California with his American wife of ten years.